A DALES COUNTRYSIDE COOKBOOK

The Dales Countryside Museum at Hawes in Wensleydale, North Yorkshire opened in 1979. The Upper Dales Folk Museum as it was then known was created in order to exhibit the collection presented to the County in 1972 by Marie Hartley and Joan Ingilby. They collected these artefacts during research for their books about this area. Their invaluable foresight rescued many items which were no longer in use, their research recorded just in time many fast-disappearing crafts and traditions.

Now the museum has been re-named and continues to grow. The Friends of the Dales Countryside Museum is a registered charity formed in 1982. Members meet several times a year for lectures, fund-raising events, outings - and an annual spring-clean of the museum (the latter being one of the best possible ways of becoming familiar with the exhibits!).

PROCEEDS FROM THE SALE OF THIS BOOK WILL GO TO THE
MUSEUM DEVELOPMENT FUND

Published 1993 by the Friends of the Dales Countryside Museum
The Dales Countryside Museum Hawes North Yorkshire DL8 3NT
Text and Illustrations © 1993 Janet Rawlins Leyland.
Typesetting and many of the illustrations were designed by Janet Rawlins on an Apple Macintosh. The typeface is New Century Schoolbook.
Printing and binding by William Sessions Limited The Ebor Press York
ISBN 0 9521111 1 X

A DALES COUNTRYSIDE

In four Sections:
I Food from the Past
II Traditional Dales Food
III Food from the Dales Countryside
IV Food for Today

Compiled and Illustrated by
Janet Rawlins

Janet Rawlins

Published by The Friends of
the Dales Countryside Museum

To Peter

CONTENTS

West End House, Askrigg 1993

*Eleven years ago we were working on this house, said to be over 500
years old and in which my husband Peter Leyland's maternal family
have lived for the past 150 years. David Hall recognised the huge beam
in the kitchen as a bressumer beam, which would have supported a fire
hood. He suggested we should investigate an oddly thick wall to the
side, and sure enough this contained a bee-hive bread oven. Beside the
big fireplace in the main living room, always called the 'house' (fire-
house), we uncovered spaces in the wall. These were for salt and spice
cupboards and would have had carved wooden doors. Since then I have
been curious to know more about the way the people who lived here,
and in the rest of the upper dales, cooked and ate.*

*There is a strong feeling of continuity in this area well illustrated for
me when visiting James and Peg Scarr just a mile up the dale. (James
shares with my husband the same great grandfather Azariah
Chapman, who farmed at West End House). They gave us a root of
Lemon Balm from their garden in front of Coleby Hall. This herb was
introduced by the Romans, cultivated in the monasteries and favoured
by Elizabethan and Jacobean gardeners. Across the river we could see
the outline of the Roman fort at Bainbridge; in the field over the road
the site of Fors Abbey; behind us was Coleby's handsome 1655 façade.*

*I am singularly unqualified to compile a cookbook, being a fairly
spasmodic cook, a hopeless pastry maker - unforgivable in this part of
the country - and a cowardly carnivore. I am half-way to being
vegetarian and prefer to deal with meat only if it is quite a long way
from being recognisable as animal. And worst of all I'm an off-comer
from the West Riding! Neither am I a historian nor a botanist.
However I do like food, and I dearly love these upper dales. As an artist
I enjoy working with colours and textures hence an interest in salads,*

herbs, berries and flowers. I confess that unlike professional cookery writers I have not tested every recipe and take no responsibility for calamities . . . However I hope that like me you will fancy deciphering and trying out some of the old recipes.

Yorkshire hospitality is well known, and the upper dales of Wensleydale, Swaledale and Wharfedale abound in talented cooks. I would like to thank the people who have generously contributed recipes.

Writing as 'Anne the still-room Maid,' Mrs Margaret Hopper produced a number of booklets from the 1950s to the 1970s which are still treasured by many local people. She was one of those responsible for the construction of a mediæval kitchen at Bolton Castle in 1951. Many of the items from this kitchen are now in the Dales Countryside Museum. One of her daughters, Ann Holubecki, is Vice-Chairman of the Friends of the Museum and has kindly let me use a number of the recipes. Josephine Hopper, another daughter, allowed me to borrow from her vast collection of historical cookbooks which have been invaluable for research.

I would like to thank Marie Hartley and Joan Ingilby for going through the manuscript - and for permitting me to quote from and obtain information from their books, William Mayne for help with the computer and photocopying, and my husband Peter, who put up with my one-track-mindedness for several months, and then valiantly proof-read and dealt with inconsistencies like three different abbreviations for teaspoon! My thanks also to Mary Bell for her memories of Haytime and Pig Killing, to Edith Leyland for her reminiscences of life in a village shop, Jane Gardam and William Mayne whose books have provided appropriate quotations and Roger Phillips for letting me use recipes from his book 'Wild Food'. And to June Hall, Robin and Denny Minnitt and Richard and Barbara Gardner.

Landscape Illustrations

SECTION I

FOOD
FROM THE PAST

The bare-boned landscape of these upper dales means that we can see evidence of former occupation all around us. The earliest visitors after the Ice Age were the Mesolithic people around 6,000BC, who used flint and bone implements (they were great fishers, using bone harpoons). At first there were reindeer, arctic fox and hare, then wild cattle, brown bear, red deer, wolf, fox and smaller mammals, so some of the meat eaten by these first dalesmen would be unfamiliar to us.

As the climate improved hazel, pine and birch woodland clothed the hillsides. The first Neolithic tribes began to settle around 3,500BC, they kept sheep, dogs, cattle and goats, grew grains and made cooking pots. On Addlebrough (which I can see as I write) and just beyond, are late Neolithic, Bronze Age, Iron Age and later remains. It does help to get time in perspective. There are pre-historic burial sites, hut circles, enclosures, cooking sites and possible food storage structures to be seen - if you know what you are looking for!

When Semerwater was lowered in the 1930s evidence of prehistoric occupation was found dating from Mesolithic times onward (the legend of the lost city may well have originated in the destruction of a settlement in a flood). I picked up a flint arrow-head on the shore there one day, warm from the sun. It seemed warm as though it had just left the hand of its maker - yet he probably lost it over 4,000 years ago.

There would have been an abundant supply of fish 'on the doorstep'; various edible marsh plants and roots; the garlic flavours of rocambole and ramsons, leaves, seeds, berries, and fungi. Animals would be easy prey as they came to the lake to drink. A magnificent bronze spearhead found on the shore is now in the Dales Countryside Museum, together with numerous flint and chert arrow points.

By the Early Bronze Age there were settled farms where wheat and barley were cultivated. Around 400 - 500BC oats, which are better suited to thin soils and the harsher climate, were being grown so it seems likely that havercake and porridge have been familiar fare in the dales for more than 2,000 years

The numerous lynchets along the fell sides in Wensleydale and Wharfedale show where land has been ploughed from late pre-historic to mediaeval times. Anglian farmers came around 600 to 800AD, life gradually became more settled and clusters of farms grew into villages. Cottagers would keep a pig and a few hens.

The Norse settlers came from the west, from Ireland, around the 10th century and settled in the wilder hilly areas west of Askrigg. Norse place-names abound, as do many Norse-derivative dialect words, and the 'long house' plan of the farmhouses. Their farming was similar to that carried on today, with the breeding of sheep and cattle.

The Roman road came over from Lancaster to the fort (once thought to be Bracchium, now more probably Virosidum) at Bainbridge, which was occupied on and off for the first four centuries A.D. and housed 500 soldiers. There are remains of a 4th century farm on the hillside close by and no doubt the farmers there would have been pressed into providing food, but an enormous amount must have been needed to feed such numbers. The Romans enjoyed the sport of hunting, especially the wild boar, and shot game birds with bows and arrows. They are credited -or blamed- for introducing ground elder to this country, which they ate as a vegetable. They also introduced Fat Hen, which they cooked like spinach (it still grows profusely on roadsides near Catterick). Provisions were brought from far afield, wine, oil, spices and flavourings coming from Italy. Numerous oyster shells have been excavated, it would be a great effort to bring them up into the wilds of Wensleydale (probably up the Ouse from York) but oysters were transported in barrels of brine even to Rome. Grain was stored in long stone granaries and numerous stone querns for grinding have been found.

The Roman breakfast was a fairly simple affair of bread soaked in wine and water. In towns and villas the other meals were elaborate, highly spiced and varied. In such an outpost as Virosidum perhaps not, but we will imagine a feast when one Julius Martinus, a centurion who was there in 208 A.D. entertained some visiting dignitaries - perhaps the owners of the Romano British villa at Middleham! Then the menu could have included snails fattened in milk; pheasants; sucking pig; oysters; trout; chicken; venison; fritters,

11

lettuce and elderberries.

The Romans used a good deal of a flavouring known as liquamen, (or garum) which was manufactured much as Worcestershire sauce is today. Here is a much-simplified recipe, the real stuff was fermented for many months.

LIQUAMEN

3 tablesp red wine	3 oz salt
½ pt water	3 anchovy fillets
1 level teasp dried oregano	

Place wine, salt and water in saucepan. Chop anchovies and add with oregano. Bring to boil, stirring, then simmer gently 10 mins. Cool, strain and bottle.

Roman meals took much the same form as nowadays, with a starter a main course and a dessert, but there would be numerous dishes offered at each course. Here is an up-dated and more restrained menu for four. (*I don't know whether they had introduced cucumbers or chicory into Britain so this first recipe cheats a bit!)*

GUSTATIO (Hors d'oevre)

4 oz button mushrooms
2 tablesp red wine
½ teasp ground coriander
Bring all to boil in a small pan and cook, shaking the pan occasionally, until the liquid is almost all gone. Cool.

Peel and slice **half a cucumber.** Mix **2 teasp clear honey, pinch white pepper , 2 teasp liquamen, 2 tablesp wine vinegar** together and pour over cucumber.

Slice 1 **head of chicory.** Peel and chop 1 **small onion,** mix with 1 **tablesp cooking oil** and 2 **tablesp white wine,** pour this dressing over the **chicory.**

Chill all three salads for about 2 hours.

MENSA PRIMA

PULLUS PARTICUS

1 medium chicken	1 teasp dried lovage
2 teasp caraway seeds	1 tablesp liquamen
¼ pt white wine	2 level teasp cornflour
1 tablesp water	
½ teasp white pepper	

Combine all ingredients except cornflour and water, pour over chicken in an ovenproof casserole and cook in moderate hot oven 190ºC 375ºF gas 5 about 1 and quarter hours. Remove lid for last 30 mins to brown. Remove chicken and keep warm while blending cornflour and water and adding to the chicken juices (after pouring off most of the fat). Stir until thickened then pour over chicken.

CYMA ET PORRI
(Cabbage and Leeks with spices)

1 small green cabbage	3 leeks
1 teasp liquamen	1 tablesp oil
1 tablesp white wine	½ teasp ground cumin
¼ teasp pepper	½ teasp caraway seed
¼ teasp ground coriander	

Shred cabbage. Trim and wash leeks, halving lengthwise. Steam about 5 minutes then arrange in ovenproof dish, leeks on top. Mix remaining ingredients, pour over and bake half an hour.

DULCIA DOMESTICA

8 oz box of dates	pinch salt
2 oz blanched almonds, or walnuts	
6 tablesp clear honey	

Stone dates then stuff with 2 almonds or a piece of walnut. Heat honey in small pan, add dates, cook gently about 3 mins, spooning honey over. Serve warm.

PANIS DULCIS

Remove crusts from thick slices of white bread and cut into cubes.
Soak in milk for 10 mins. Fry the cubes in half an inch of hot oil until
pale gold. Drain on kitchen paper and serve with warmed honey
poured over.

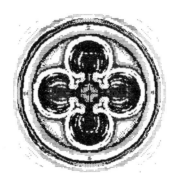

The Cistercian monks came to Fors, between Askrigg and
Bainbridge, in 1145. It was a wild forested area reserved for
hunting, but the monks were permitted to take deer which had been
mauled by wolves! They bred sheep, and made cheese from ewes
milk, but after 11 years they moved down the dale to a more
sheltered place, still on the banks of the river Yore, (hence Jorvallis,
meaning Yore Vale, which became Jervaulx). This is the first time
the making of cheese in Wensleydale is recorded, the monks of Fors
may well have brought the recipe from France. But cheesemaking is
recorded in other parts long before this, and I would suspect that the
Anglian and Norse settlers may have had some form of cheesemaking
skills.

The monasteries owned vast tracts of land on the upland fells
and became skilled sheep and cattle farmers, improving the breeds
and making quantities of cheese. They had Guest Houses where
travellers could obtain food and shelter. With their fish ponds,
apiaries, herbs and farming skills the monks must have been
admirable hosts. There are still plants such as vipers bugloss
descendants of their medicinal and flavouring herbs, growing among
the ruins at Jervaulx Abbey.

Soon after the monks retreated from Fors a new village,
Bainbridge, was created nearby to house twelve foresters. By 1280
Bainbridge had thirteen farms in the Forest of Wensleydale.

"It is described as having a capital messuage, 34 acres of arable land, 200 acres of meadow, a water mill, an oven, and a brewery - an early picture of a dales village"
from Marie Hartley and Joan Ingilby's 'Yorkshire Village'

This gives a picture of a surprisingly settled life. The communal oven would be of the 'igloo' type still seen in places like Cyprus. The foresters also kept pigs which fed on acorns and beech mast (proving that there were some substantial trees, not just the hazel and hawthorn scrub which still survives along the valley sides) and guided strangers through the forest (hence the continuing tradition of the Bainbridge Hornblower).

One can imagine the scene when the lords of Richmond and Middleham came to hunt deer and wild boar. Did the villagers prepare a mid-day meal for them? Bread and oatcake from the oven; ale from the brewery; cheese, pork, fungi, brambles? Did the successful hunters leave behind any of their 'bag'? Poaching was punishable by death so they would otherwise get no chance to taste venison. However innards - numbles or humbles - were made into pies for the lower orders, hence the saying 'eating humble pie'.

The church decreed that only fish should be eaten on Fridays, and until late in mediæval times on Saturdays and Wednesdays as well, also throughout Lent when eggs and dairy foods were also forbidden. Perhaps it was one way of arresting the gluttony of the wealthy, but it must have caused great hardship amongst the poor in areas such as these dales so far from the sea. Salt cod and sometimes pickled and kippered herring were the only sea fish available. These would be brought by pack horse the 80 miles or so from the East coast, 40 from the West.

The fish in the river belonged to the landowners. Salmon came up the Ure as far as Aysgarth falls, and up the Clough into Garsdale until well into this century. Trout and grayling were plentiful, and eels were caught near Middleham until recent times weighing up to three and a half pounds.

15

Eels were skinned and boiled, stewed, or spatchcocked by being skewered (either into a circle or back and forth), egg-and-breadcrumbed and grilled.

The majority of people would live on bread, oatcake, and cheese. They made pottages, mish-mashes and broths of vegetables, herbs, cabbage, beans, peas and onions, with pounded grains and just occasionally some meat. Fat hen was grown as a vegetable and it is still found growing wherever there has been habitation, even in farmyards only deserted in recent years. The roots of silverweed were boiled or baked like parsnip or sometimes dried and ground for gruel (the leaves were also used as a cooling lining to the shoes of foot soldiers!) Flummery was made from oatmeal boiled in milk and flavoured with various seasonings.

When a market was granted at Wensley in 1202, trading would make possible a wider choice.

Middleham Castle, built first as a motte-and-bailey castle after the Norman Conquest, and then the present stone keep around 1170, dominated the lower dale. In the 13th century when the Nevilles were a powerful family and young Richard Duke of Gloucester spent his boyhood there, it would be the scene of some gargantuan feasts.

The *FORME OF CURY*, one of the earliest recipe books was written about 1390 at the request of Richard II. It is more than likely that it would be in use at Middleham Castle. The following menu for a feast was not unusual:

First course- Venison, broth, boar's heads, roast meat, roast swans and peacocks, roast pigs, custard with dried fruit, 'and a soltete' (a fancy edible table decoration, possibly a model of the castle).

Second course- Jellied soup, chicken & almond stew, roast pigs, cranes, pheasants, chickens, rabbits. Bream, tarts, and another soltete.

Third course- Almond soup, Lombardy stew, roast venison, chicken, rabbits, quails, larks, an egg & ginger tart, jelly, sweetmeats....and a soltete.

TART De BRYMLENT

"Take fyges and raysons and waiſſe hem in wyne and grinde hem ſmale with apples and peres clene ypiked; take hem up and caſt hem in a pot with wyne and ſugar take ſalwar ſalmon yſode other codling other haddock and bray hem ſmale and do thereto white powders and hool ſpices and ſalt and ſeeth it and whanneit is ſode ynowf take it up and do it in a veſſel and lat it kele. Make a coffyn an ynche depe and do the fars therein plant it bove with prunes and damsyns take the ſtones out and with dates quarte rede and piked clean and cover the coffyn and bak it wel and ſerve it forth."

Which is roughly **A MID-LENTEN TART**

pastry for 10" pie, with lid.

1 oz butter	2 peeled & sliced pears
8 fl oz white wine	2 peeled & sliced apples
2 tablesp lemon juice	1 oz brown sugar
4 oz raisins	10 prunes, chopped

6 dates, 6 figs, chopped
2 tablesp milk
1½ lbs fish - salmon, cod, or haddock, cut into chunks,
sprinkled with salt and lemon juice
1 dessertsp redcurrant jelly
pinch of cloves, nutmeg & cinnamon

Bake pastry base blind for 10 mins. In a heavy based frying pan melt butter, coat apple & pear slices and stir. Add dried fruits, wine, lemon juice, sugar & spices, cover & simmer 10 mins or so. Remove fresh fruit and reduce liquid by fast-boiling. Paint the cooled pie shell with redcurrant jelly. Put the chunks of fish over the pastry, cover with the fresh and dried fruit. Cover with pastry lid, flute edges and decorate with pastry fish. Paint over with milk. Bake at 375° for 30-40 mins.
An adaptation of Lorna Sass's version in 'To the King's Taste'

(And this one, reminiscent of fish-and- chip shop scraps!)
CRYSPEY (1430)   Take whyte of eggs, mylke and floure and beat it together draw it through a ſtraynour ſo that it be running and not too ſtyff. Caſte thereto ſugare and ſalte then take a diſſhe full of freſh greece boyling and put thy hand into the batter, let the batter runne down thy fingers into the diſſhe. When it is done enough take a ſkymmer, take it up and lette all the greece runne out. Put it in a diſſhe and caſte ſugar thereon.

17

GARLIC was eaten profusely, both for its medicinal properties, and cooked as a vegetable. They recommended chewing garden mint or sipping vinegar afterwards to get rid of the smell - but I imagine that one more smell in those days would hardly matter!

In 1379 Richard, Lord Scrope began the building of Bolton Castle, which took 18 years. Said to be originally plastered white, it must have been an impressive sight and would easily be seen from Middleham - a bit of keeping-up-with-the-Nevilles!

The meals no doubt would also rival their neighbours. The lists of food prepared for meals in this period are quite overwhelming, every imaginable kind of meat and fowl. As well as the game and domestic fowl, the elaborately garnished peacocks and swans, they ate bustard, crane, heron, gull, curlew, egret, quail, plover, snipe, lapwing, thrush, bittern and greenfinch and blackbird (the four and twenty in the pie is not just a nursery rhyme, it was a popular way to amuse ones guests when the birds were packed alive into a previously baked crust - another soltete). Food was highly spiced, often to disguise meat that was less than fresh! Hardly any vegetables appear in these menus, they were thought to cause wind and were only used in soups and broths. Fruit was served at the end of the meal but generally cooked in pies, fresh fruit was regarded with suspicion.

Trenchers (thick slices of stale, unleavened bread) were used as plates. When too sodden with gravy they were replaced and the bread collected in baskets to give to the poor. (Our convention of breaking, not biting, our dinner rolls comes through from this time.) Guests brought their own knives and spoons - forks did not come into general use until the 17th century. There was a great fear among the nobility of being poisoned, so a 'taster' had to test each dish. Unicorn's horn was considered a safe test for poison, so cups were made containing a piece of horn. *(I wonder where it came from?!)*

COCKYNTRICE   (1430)

Take a cockerel and ſcald him and draw him clene and ſmite him in two acroſs the waſte. Take a pig and ſcald him and draw him in the ſame manner ſmite him in two acroſs the waſte. Take a nedel and threde and ſew the fore part of the pigge to the hinder part of the cockerel and the hinder part of the pigge to the fore part of the cockerel and then ſtuff him as thou ſtuffesſt a pigge. Put him on a ſpitte and roſt him and when he is enough gild him with yolks of egg and powdered ginger and ſaffron and jus of parsley. Serve it forth for a royale meat.

Dorothy Hartley gave a recipe as recently as 1954 saying "This 'antient conceit' uses up elderly fowl or rabbit well, and makes a decorative dish that delights children (for parties)........."
I think most childrens' tastes have changed in the past forty years!

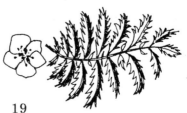

19

LECHE LUMBARD   Date Roll

800 g (1¾ lb) block of dates
425 ml (¾ pt) white wine
75 g (3 oz) soft brown sugar   pinch mixed spice
½ teasp each of cinnamon and ground ginger
5 hard boiled egg yolks   3 slices brown bread
60 ml (4 tablesp) sweet red wine

The pestle and mortar would have been hard work, but if you have a food processor this is an easy one. First make breadcrumbs from the slices. Put the broken-up dates, wine and sugar in a pan and cook gently until mushy. Process until almost smooth, adding egg yolks, ginger and cinnamon, then enough breadcrumbs to make a firm mixture. Roll it into a 2" diameter sausage and chill (it keeps well in the fridge). Gently heat the red wine with a pinch of spice, then cool and serve with thin slices of the date mixture.

Although we are told that few vegetables were eaten at this time, here is a 15th century salad that can teach us a thing or two, and could have been in the Countryside section - but I love the spelling!

Buddys of ſtanmarche (alexanders), vyolette flourez, parceley, red myntes, ſyves, creſſe of Boleyne, purſelane, ramſons, clamyntes, primeroſe buddus, dayſes, rapounſes, daundelion, rokette, red nettel, borage flourez, croppus of red fenelle, seleſtryve, chykenwede.

PECOCK ROSTED   (1450)

Take a pecock; breke his necke and kutte his throte And fle him, and ſkin him, the ſkin and fethurs together. And the hede ſhall ſtill be to the necke. Roſt him and ſet the bone of the neck aboue the breaſt as he was wonte to ſitte a-lyve, And aboue the legges to the body, as he was wonte to ſitte a-lyve; and when he is roſted ynowe take him of And let him kele; And then wynde the ſkyn with the fethurs and the tail abought the body and ſerve it forth as he were alyve; or elles pull him dry, And roſt him, and ſerue him as thou doſt a hen.

Unlike our familiar sweet cornflour pudding the original blancmange was made from white meats.

Blanc-Mang

"Take capons and ſeeth them thenne take hem up; take almandes blanced grynd hem and alay hem up with the ſame broth; caſt the mylk in a pot waiſſe rais and do thereto and lat it ſeethe, thanne take brawn of caponns, teere it ſmall and do thereto; take whyte greece ſugar and ſalt and caſt thereinne, lat it seethe, then meſs it forth and florish it with aneys in confit and with almandes fryed in oyle and serve it forth."

BLANC-MANGE

2 large chicken breasts	salt
1 pt water	8 oz rice
4 oz blanched almonds	½ oz butter
1 dessertsp light brown sugar	

Boil the chicken in the salted water for 15 mins or so until tender. Grind almonds in a blender, adding the water in which the chicken was cooked. Leave about 10 mins, then pour into a saucepan, add the rice, sugar, butter and 1 teasp salt. Chop the chicken and add to the rice when almost cooked. Finish cooking, pile into serving dish. *Alternatively this could then be all be whizzed in the blender to make a more authentic smooth purée.* Garnish with 1 oz flaked almonds (fried in oil) and chopped green sweet cicely seeds or crushed aniseed.

Adapted from 'To the King's Taste" by Lorna Sass

Mary Queen of Scots was imprisoned at Bolton Castle from the 13th of July 1568 to the 26th of January 1569. She brought a retinue of 40 servants (half had to be housed in the village). Queen Elizabeth sent household utensils and 'necessaries incident to dinners' Venison was sent each week, and 'she was allowed to hunt'. It must have called for great organisation of the castle brewhouses and bakehouses (still to be seen) and one can imagine the relief of the cooks when she left!

(In 1645 the parliamentary forces were besieged there and were 'reduced to eating horseflesh'. Soon afterwards it became untenable, and the great castle's later indignity was to be divided up into cottages and workshops, when even humbler fare was cooked in the huge fireplaces.)

Drawn from a copy of Mary Queen of Scots sand glass which timed three, four and five minutes. She must have liked her eggs well done!

James Metcalfe fought with Sir Richard le Scrope at Agincourt, and on his return was granted the estate of Nappa, where he built Nappa Hall in about 1459.

Later generations of Metcalfes married well, and by the mid-16th century were a powerful local family. Let us imagine that Sir Christopher and Lady Metcalfe had invited guests to dinner in the panelled hall with its minstrels gallery.

The old trestle tables were still being used for the servants, but the family and guests would sit at a sturdy oak table covered with a linen cloth. Silver plates replaced the trenchers of yore (wood for the servants) and for this special occasion the new Venetian glass goblets were to be brought out. The children had gone to the riverside to gather meadowsweet and other scented herbs to strew over the stone-flagged floor.

Lady Metcalfe was particularly proud of her lettuces in the new garden with its pattern of herbs, and the green vegetables which were now becoming popular. The servants had been down the dale to Wensley market for provisions; dried fruits, flour and root vegetables. (Soon afterwards in 1563 the plague devastated Wensley. The market was never to recover. In 1587 Askrigg was granted a market charter.) There were oranges at Wensley this week; and loaves of sugar, still a rarity but becoming popular. Spices were extremely expensive, they had bought cinnamon, cloves, mace, nutmeg and ginger. In the kitchen the meats were roasting on a turning spit. Apart from the use of sugar the menu had changed little over the past hundred years and still consisted of numerous courses (but guests would take a little of what they fancied, it was no longer considered obligatory to over-eat). Bread and cakes had been baked; the best white wheat made into manchet loaves, some larger loaves of the second quality flour (known as cheat), and brown loaves for the servants.

How to Make FARTES OF PORTINGALE

Take a piece of leg of mutton. Mince it ſmal and ſeason it with cloves, mace , pepper and ſalt, and Dates minced with currants: then roll it into round rolles, and ſo into little balles, and ſo boyle them in a little beef broth and ſo ſerve them forth.

(Fartes pronounced fart<u>ess</u> !)

from The Good Huſwife's Handmaid

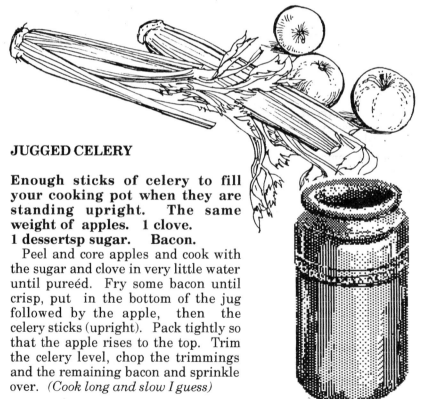

JUGGED CELERY

Enough sticks of celery to fill your cooking pot when they are standing upright. The same weight of apples. 1 clove. 1 dessertsp sugar. Bacon.

Peel and core apples and cook with the sugar and clove in very little water until pureéd. Fry some bacon until crisp, put in the bottom of the jug followed by the apple, then the celery sticks (upright). Pack tightly so that the apple rises to the top. Trim the celery level, chop the trimmings and the remaining bacon and sprinkle over. *(Cook long and slow I guess)*

24

This **'COMPOST'** *from 1513 seems to be a forerunner of our chutney.*
Take rote of parſel, paſternak of raſens, ſcrape hem and waiſſhe
hem clene, take rapes and caboches ypared and icorne, take an
earthen pane with clene water, and ſet it on the fire; caſt all this
threinne, when they buth boiled caſt into peeres and parboile him
wele; take thiſe thinynges up and lat it kele on a fair cloth. Do
thereto ſalt whan it is cold in a veſſel, take vynegar and powdor and
ſafron and do thereto and lat alle thiſe thynges lye threinne al nygt
other al day; take wyne greke and hony claryfyed togider lumbarde
muſtard and raiſons corance al hool and grynde powdor of canal,
powdor douce and aneys hole and fenell seed; take alle thiſs thynges
and caſt togyder in a pot of erthe and take thereof whan thou wilt
and ſerve it forth. *(rape - turnip, caboches - cabbages, corance -
currants)*

CHICKEN WITH GOOSEBERRY SAUCE

1 chicken   1 carrot   1 onion   1 stick celery
bunch of parsley   knot of thyme
Cover chicken with cold water, add chopped vegetables and herbs.
bring to boil, remove scum, then simmer gently for 1 to 2 hours until
tender.
make a sauce with:
      a handful of gooseberries
      parsley, thyme, mace,   salt and pepper
      ½ pt (or a little less) white wine
      chicken stock   ¼ pt cream

Chop gooseberries and herbs, simmer in the wine plus some of the
chicken stock for half an hour or so to reduce to a fairly thick sauce.
Blend and/or sieve, reheat gently then add the cream (or a nut of
butter).

For a true 16th century dish slice the chicken and serve on a bed of
'sippets' - toasted bread slices - with the sauce poured over.
Alternatively serve with rice.

TO MAKE A DYSCHEFULL OF SNOWE (1575)

Take a pottell of ſwete thicke creame and the whytes of eyghte egges and beate them altogether wyth a ſpone. Then putte them in youre cream and a ſaucerfull of Roſewater and a dyſhe full of ſuger wyth all. Then take a ſtycke and make it cleane and then cutte it in the ende foure-ſquare, and therwith beate all the aforeſayde things together, and ever as it ryſeth take it off and put it into a Collaunder. This done take one apple and ſet it in the myddes of it and a thicke buſhe of Roſemary and ſet it in the myddes of the platter therewith. Then caſt your Snowe uppon the Roſemarie and fyll your platter therwith. And yf you have ſome waſers caſte ſome in wyth all and thus ſerve them forthe.

from A Proper Newe Booke of Cookerye
(It is rare to be given quantities - a pottel was a gallon, a saucer and a dish the forerunners of the American cup measure?) Try baking the apple!

The Elizabethan Mincemeat pie contained, as its name would suggest, minced meat - it was only in the late 19th century that the meat disappeared altogether, although I have found a "mincemeat-without-meat" in a book of 1710

TO MAKE MINST PIES

Take you veal and perboil it a little, or mutton. Then ſet it a cooling: and when it is colde, take three pound of ſuit to a legge of mutton, or fower pound to a fillet of Veale, and then mince them

26

ſmall by themſelves, or together whether you will. Then take to ſeaſon them halfe an unce of Sinamon, a little pepper, as much ſalt as you think will ſeaſon them, either to the mutton or to the Veale, take eight yolkes of Egges when they be hard, half a pinte of roſewater full measure, halfe a pound of ſuger. Then ſtrain the Yolkes with the roſewater and the Suger and mingle it with your meats. If ye have any Orrenges or Lemmans you must take two of them, and take the pilles very thin and mince them very ſmalle, and put them in a pound of currans, ſix dates, half a pound of prunes. Lay Currans and Dates upon the top of your meate. You muſt take two or three Pomewaters or Wardens and mince with your meat. . . ; if you will make a good cruſt put in three or foure yolkes of eggs, a little Roſewater, and a good deal of Suger.

from the Good Hous-wives Treasurie

TO BOYLE A CAPON WITH ORENGES
After Miſtreſs Duffield's Way

Take a capon and boyle it with Veale, or with a good marie bone, or what your fancy is. Then take a good quantitie of that broth, and put it in an earthen pot by it ſelf, and put thereto a good handfull of Currans, and as manie Prunes, and a few whole maces, and ſome Marie, and put to this broth a good quantitie of white wine or of Clarret, and ſo let them ſethe ſoftly together: Then take your Orenges, and with a knife ſcrape all the filthineſſe of the outſide of them. Then cut them in the middeſt, and wring out the juyce of three or foure of them, put the juyce into your broth with the reſt of your ſtuffe. Then ſlice your Orenges thinne, and have uppon the fire ready a ſkillet of faire ſeething water, and put your ſliced oranges into the water and when that water is bitter have more readie, and ſo change them ſtill as long as you can find great bitterneſs in the water, which will be five or ſeven times or more. If you need: then take them from the water and let that runne cleane from them: then put close Orenges into your potte with your broth, and ſo let them ſtew together till your capon be readie. Then make your ſops with this broth, and caſt on a

27

little Sinamon, Ginger and Sugar, and upon this lay your capon, and some of your oranges upon it, and some of your Marie, and towarde the end of the boyling of your broth, put in a little Vergious, if you think best.

Mistress Duffeld will have used Seville oranges hence the need to remove bitterness. It must have been an expensive dish! Marie is rosemary, and vergious - verjuice - is tart crab-apple juice, often used in place of vinegar.

The 17th Century saw the building of a number of substantial stone houses. In 1655 John Coleby (from a Suffolk family of some standing) built Coleby Hall which is still a handsome landmark on the hillside between Bainbridge and Askrigg. Architectural fashions were slow to filter to these parts and the house has more a feel of an Elizabethan manor house. Lady Anne Clifford stayed a night there on two occasions when travelling between her Pendragon Castle in Mallerstang, and Skipton Castle. In 1663 she had stayed at "My Cozen Mr Thomas Metcalfe's house at Nappa", then in 1666 (and again the following year) she stayed at Coleby Hall.

"And so over Cotter and those dangerous Wayes into one Mr John Colebys House near Bambrigg in Winsdale, where I lay that night with my women Servants and some 3 of my Menservants, my other servants lying at Askrigg and Bambrigg"

Like the house, Lady Anne was of a former age and liked to travel by coach or litter with a retinue of servants. She was by then

28

seventy six and after her hazardous journey might well have been glad of a posset and a fairly early night! However, one can imagine that John Coleby would wish to show off his famous visitor by inviting a few guests.

So we can picture the scene as they prepared for the supper that evening. The main meal would normally be served at mid-day but on this occasion it was to be at 5.30, supper time. Extra helpers were brought in from the villages, probably the very folk who would provide Lady Anne's servants with beds that night. Guests had been invited from among the 'worthies' of the neighbourhood, including the Thornton family from West End in Askrigg. (Young Simon Thornton was later to marry Margaret Coleby).

Preparations had begun several days ahead with the killing of a pig; now lamb, several chickens, grouse and trout were being cooked on spits and in pots. An enormous cauldron simmered, hanging on a reckan from the crane beside one of the three vast fireplaces. Inside the cauldron were packed various dishes standing on a perforated wooden board: meats sealed inside jars; puddings hung in cloths; a piece of bacon down beneath the board wrapped in flour-and-water paste and a linen cloth. Parsnips, carrots and leeks were being washed by a lad down at the waterfall, along with a few of the newly-favoured vegetables, potatoes.

The long oak table in the hall was laid with pewter plates, the family silver goblets, knives, spoons, and the Coleby's latest acquisition, a set of forks. In honour of the forthcoming visit Mistress Coleby had bought a bag of the new coffee beans. She was a little nervous as she was not quite sure how to deal with them. Lady Anne would surely prefer hot chocolate, certainly at breakfast, and at supper they were to have wine in which lemon balm had been steeping - a most refreshing drink.

All summer there had been conserve and pickle making in the Coleby kitchen, along with the salting of beans and hams, the smoking of fish, drying of herbs and fruit, and candying of flowers. Raspberry and gooseberry jellies were being set into colourful moulds.

The children were down where Grange Beck meets the Yore with nets, a piece of liver on a string, and instructions to catch one hundred crayfish.

TO BUTTER CRAWFISH (Elinor Fettiplace)

Boyl the Crawfish and pick the fish out of the bodys tails and claws then take to an Hundred two or three spoonfulls of water and as much white wine a Blade of Mace or a little nutmeg a little salt and Lemmon peel let it simmer together then put in the Crawfish and shake e'm together and when they are through hot put in half a qr of a pd of Butter keep e'm shaking till the butter be melted then put in a little juice of Lemon: you may if you please boyl the shells in the water you put in.

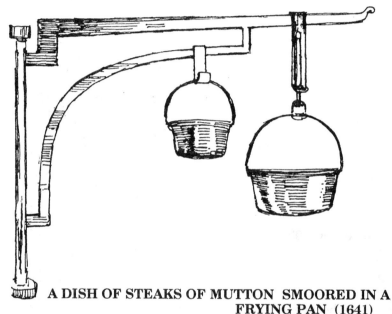

A DISH OF STEAKS OF MUTTON SMOORED IN A FRYING PAN (1641)

Take your leg of mutton and cut into ſteakes and put into a frying panne with a pint of white wine. Smoore them ſomewhat brown. Then put into a pipkin. Cut a lemon in ſlices and throw it in. Then take a good quantity of butter and hold it over the fire. When it is ready to fry put in a handful of parſley, and when it is fryed put it into the pipkin with the mutton and boyl all together. The diſh ſhould be garnished with cinnamon, ſugar, and ſliced lemons.

(Pipkin - a saucepan on legs to stand over the embers.)

from A New Book of Cookerie by John Murrel

30

GUSSET or Pottage (1575)

Take the broth of capons and put it in a faire chafer; then take a dozen or fifteen egges and ſtir them all together, white and all. Then grate a farthing white loaf as ſmall as ye can and mince it with the egges all together and put to them ſalt and a good quantity of Saffron. As ye put in youre egges put into your broth Savery, marjoram, parceley chopt ſmall and when ye are ready to eat your dinner set the chafer on the fire with the broth and let it boil a little. Then put in your egges. The less boyling it hath the more tender it will be. *from A Proper Newe Booke of Cookerye*

To make a Tart of Borage Flowers
Take Borage flowers and perboyle them tender, then ſtrayne them wyth the yolkes of four egges, and ſwet curdes, or elſe take three or four apples, and perboyle wythal and ſtrayne them with ſwete butter and a little mace and so bake it

To make a Tart of Marigolds, Primroses or Cowslips.
Take the ſame ſtuff to euery of them that you do to the tarte of borage and the same ceaſonynge.
from A Proper Newe booke of Cookerye

Pour boiling water over the flower heads, then drain. (They could be frozen and used when required.) Use one of the cheesecake recipes (page 74 or 131) but leave out the dried fruit, substitute mace for nutmeg and use 3 separated eggs, folding in the beaten whites.

31

A dish for a fish-day, an odd mixture for today's taste. Spices and dried fruits would still be very expensive, and sugar a fairly new treat, so one wonders if they were included into all-and-everything more as a matter of showing off. A warden is a pear suitable for cooking, a coffin a pastry case.

A HERRING PYE

Take white pickled Herrings of one nights watering, and boyl them a little. Then take off the ſkin, and take onely the backs of them, and pick the fiſh clean from the bones. Then take a good ſtore of Raiſins of the Sun and ſtone them and put them to the fish. Then take a warden or two and pare it and ſlice it in ſmall ſlices from the core, and put it likewiſe to the fiſh. Then ſhred all as ſmall and fine as may be: then put to it a good ſtore of Currants, Sugar, Cinnamon, ſlic'd Dates and ſo put it into the coffin with a good ſtore of very ſweet Butter and ſo cover it and leave only a round vent-hole in the Top of the lid, and ſo bake it like pyes of that nature: When it is ſufficiently bak'd draw it out and take Claret Wyne and a little verjuyce Sugar Cinnamon and ſweet Butter and boyl them together: then put it in at the vent-hole and ſhake the pye a little and put it againe into the Oven for a little ſpace and ſo ſerve it up, the lid being candied over with Sugar and the ſides of the dyſhe trimmed with Sugar.
from Gervase Markham's 'The English Hus-wife'

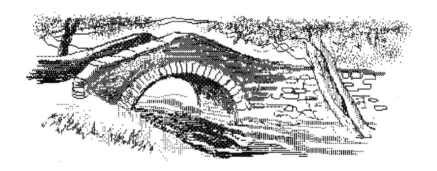

Hockett Bridge, a pack horse bridge near the site of Fors Abbey. Goods were transported by strings of pack horses until the coming of the railway in the 19th century.

TROUT WITH SWEET-SOUR SAUCE

2 trout	1 glass white wine
1 teasp sugar	knob of butter

1 scant tablesp white wine vinegar
small piece of fresh ginger root, peeled and sliced
1 dessertsp fresh herbs, chopped

Clean fish, score (or fillet if large) and pack fairly tightly into an oven-proof dish. Pour on half a cup of boiling water and heat until it bubbles. Add herbs, ginger, and the glass of wine. Cover, and poach gently for between 10 and 15 minutes.

Strain off the juices and slices of ginger. Add to this the vinegar and sugar and reduce by fast-boiling to a small cupful. Remove ginger, add a knob of butter (or some cream) and pour over the fish.

The following recipes come from
The Family Dictionary or, Household Companion compiled by Dr William Salmon in 1710. The recipes therefore must be from some years earlier than that.

This excerpt from his introduction seems appropriate.

"Thus, Reader, I preſent Thee with a miſcellaneous Collection on ſome Choice Things, excerpted with a great deal of Trouble out of a heap of other Books."

LUMBER PYE

Parboil the humbles *(see page 15)* of a Deer, free them from their Fat, put to it as much Beef ſuet, or half as much more as Meat; mince all together very ſmall, Seaſon with ſalt, Cinnamon, Cloves, Mace and Nutmeg; half a pound of Sugar, 4 pounds of large Currants, a pint of Canary, a little *D.R.W.* half a pound of candied citron, Limon and Orange peel, Dates ſtoned and ſliced; fill your pye and cloſe it; when baked, put into it 3 quarters of a pint of Canary.

BEEF TO SOUCE

Take of the Buttocks, Cheeks, and Briskets of Beef, ſeaſon any of them four Days with Pepper and Salt, roul them up as even as you can; boil them in a Cloth tyed faſt about, in Water and Salt; and when it is pretty tender, put it into a Hoop-frame to faſhion it round and upright; dry it in ſome ſmoaky Place, or in the Air, and cutting it out in Slices, ſerve it up with Sugar and Muſtard, obſerving before you dry it, to ſouce it in Water and Vinegar, and a little White-wine and Salt.

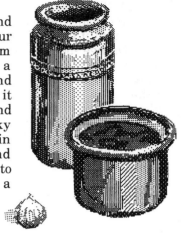

POTTAGE

To make this very excellent, nouriſhing, and conducing to Health and Strength, take the Knuckle End of a Leg of Veal, very largely cut, put it into a galoon, or ſix quarts of Spring-water, a pint of Oatmeal ſifted very fine, Pennyroyal, Parſley, Thyme, and Winter-ſavory, of each a little bundle, unſhred; alſo Sweet-marjoram, Sorrel, Violet and Marigold-leaves; you may let it ſtand a whole Night over a gentle Fire, and boil it up the next Morning, with ſome Mace, Currans, Hartshorn Shavings and Sugar; then ſtrain it, and eat it warm.

Here, an astonishingly rich
RICE PUDDING

Take half a pound of Rice, boiled in New Milk till it is ſoft; cover it cloſe, and let it be cold. Take 10 yolks and five whites of Eggs, with four ſpoonfuls of Canary, or Orange Flower Water, which beat well together; add a pint of Cream and *D.L.S.* to your Palate, a pound of melted freſh Butter, one nutmeg grated, and as much Mace pouder'd: mix altogether with the Rice, with near a pound of large Currants, which plump before they are put in: put in a Diſh lined on the bottom and ſides with Puff-paste, and ſtrew over the top a quarter of a pound or more of choice beef ſuet ſhred very ſmall; bake it, then ſerve it, *D.L.S.* ſtrewed over the top.

TAFFETY TARTS.

Take puff-paſte, or paſte made with Butter, *D.R.W.* and *D.L.S.* and Eggs, roul it out thin, put in ſlices of Pippins, and lay pieces of Candied Orange -peel in long ſlices, and *D.L.S.* then Pippins, then Orange, then *D.L.S.* ſo do till you have laid in rows as many as you will have, cloſe them, and take melted Butter, a little *D.R.W.* and waſh them with it, ſtrew *D.L.S.* upon them, and ſo bake them.

Distilled Rose Water. D? Loaf Sugar

POSSET I

Put a pint of good Milk to boil, as ſoon as it doth ſo, take it from the Fire, and let it cool a little; and when it is pretty well cooled, pour it into the Pot, wherein is about two ſpoonfuls of Sack, and four of Ale, with ſufficient Sugar diſſolved in them, ſo let it ſtand a while near the Fire, till you eat it.

POSSET II

Take two quarts of Cream, boil it with whole Spice, take twelve Eggs well beaten and ſtrained, take the Cream from the fire and ſtir in the Eggs, and as much Sugar as will ſweeten it; put in as much Sack as will make it taſte well, and ſet it on the Fire again, and let it ſtand a while; take a ladle and raiſe it up gently from the bottom of the Skillet you make it in, and ſtir it as little as you can, ſo do it till you ſeel it be thick enough; then put it into the Baſon with the Ladle gently; if you do it too much it will turn to Whey.

Dr Salmon gives a suggested Bill of fare for one meal in each month of the year, from which we can get a fair idea of what was expected of a 17th-18th Century cook. Here as examples are March and April:

March: Brawn and muſtard, freſh Neats Tongues and Udders, three Ducks, a roaſted loin of Pork, a Venison Paſty, a Stake Pye. Second Courſe; a ſide of Lanb, ſix Teal, three larded; Lambſtone Pye, two hundred of Aſparagus, a Warden Pye, Marenated Flounders, Jellies, Tarts Royal, White Ginger-bread.

April: A Biſquet, Cold Lamb, Roaſted Haunch of Veniſon, Goflins, a Turkey, Chickens, Cuſtards, Almonds dipt and dried brown. Second Courſe, a ſide of Lamb in joints, eight Turtle Doves, a cold Neats Tongue Pye, eight Pigeons, four of them larded; a collar of Beef, Lobſters, a Tanſie.

35

In 1767 Askrigg's main street changed considerably when John Pratt added the three-storey façade of his extensive house (now the Manor House and the Kings Arms). He owned racehorses, kept a pack of hounds, had a large staff of servants and, with his wife Jane, entertained a great deal. We can imagine a roisterous celebratory meal after a success at the races. He spent part of the year at Newmarket, so may well have been entertaining visitors from away and, surely, the 'Four Men' of Askrigg (records are incomplete, but John Pratt was one of this illustrious number in 1758 and 59). Meals still consisted of what to us is an enormous quantity of food and drink. Dinner started in the early afternoon and would continue, on such an occasion, for the rest of the day. Cooking therefore had to start at daybreak; great joints roasting, pottages, puddings in cloths, syllabubs and mountainous jellies.

The Pratts had pretentions, they adopted a coat of arms of three elephants heads (not registered at the college of heralds) still to be seen on a lead water-pipe head, and on memorial tablets in the church. The table would be formally laid with silver and fine glass, they would probably be among the first in the district to acquire a 'dinner service' of matching china, Their entertaining in Askrigg may not have been on quite such a grand scale as the following from Elizabeth Raffald but we can assume that, as with her menu, large quantities of meat would be served, and few if any vegetables.

36

Elizabeth Raffald's directions for a January Grand Table in 'AN EXPERIENCED ENGLISH HOUSEKEEPER' (1769) includes hare soup, a haunch of venison, duck a la mode, ox pallets, roast lamb, larded oysters, a florendine of rabbits, roast hare, potted shrimps, snipe in savoury jelly, collared pig, pistacia cream and Rocky Island! Creations such as the Rocky Island jelly are a direct descendant of the mediæval Soltete.

Her requirements for the third course show what elaborate etiquette had developed in the great houses, where the precise number of dishes served was laid down.

"I have not engraved a copper plate for a third courſe, or a cold collation, for that generally conſiſts of things extravagant; but I have endeavoured to ſet a deſſert of ſweetmeats, which the induſtrious houſewife may lay up in ſummer, at ſmall expence, and when added to what little fruit is then in ſeaſon, will make a pretty appearance after the cloth is drawn, and be entertaining to the company; before you draw your cloth, have all your ſweetmeats and fruits diſhed up in china diſhes, or fruit baſkets; and as many diſhes as you have in one courſe, ſo many baſkets or plates your deſert must have; and as my bill of fare is twenty five in each course, ſo muſt your deſſert be of the ſame number, and ſet out in the ſame manner, and as ice is very often plentiful at that time it will be eaſy to make five different ices for the middle, either to be ſerved upon a frame or without, with four plates of

37

dried fruit round them; apricots, green gages, grapes and pears; the four outward corners piſtachio nuts, prunellos, oranges and olives. The four ſquares nonpariels, pears, walnuts, and fiberts; the two in the centre betwixt the top and the bottom cheſtnuts and Portugal plumbs; for ſix long dibhes, pine apples, French plumbs, and the four brandy fruits, which are peaches, nectarines, apricots and cherries".

To Make a Rocky Island

Make a little ſtiff flummery, and put it into five fiſh moulds, wet them before you put it in, when it is ſtiff turn it out, and gild them with gold leaf, then take a deep China diſh, fill it near half full of clear calves foot jelly, and let it ſtand till it is ſet, then lay on your fiſhes, and a few ſlices of red currant jelly, cut very thin round them, then raſp a ſmall French roll, and rub it over with the white of an egg, and ſtrew it all over with ſilver bran, and glitter mixed together, ſtick ſprig of myrtle in it, and put it into the middle of your diſh, beat the white of an egg to a very high froth, then hang it on your ſprig of myrtle like ſnow, and fill your diſh to the brim with clear jelly; when you ſend it to the table put lambs or ducks upon the jelly, with either green leaves or moſs under them, with their heads towards the myrtle.
(Phew!!)

The flummery was made from 2 oz blanched almonds pounded in a mortar with a little rose water, sweetened with loaf sugar and boiled up with a pint of calves foot stock, strained, slightly cooled, added to a pint of thick cream and stirred until cold.

The following would make tasty canapés today, again from Elizabeth Raffald.

To Make a Nice Whet before Dinner

Cut ſome ſlices of bread half an inch thick, fry them in butter, but not too hard, then ſplit ſome anchovies, take out the bones, and lay half an anchovy on each piece of bread, have ready ſome Cheſhire cheese grated, and ſome chopt parsley mixt together, lay it pretty thick over the bread and anchovy, baſte it with butter, and brown it with a ſalamander; it muſt be done on the diſh you ſend it to the table.

A salamander was a long-handled iron plate which was heated in the fire then held over the food to grill it.

To Make Yorkshire Pudding to bake under Meat.

Beat four eggs with four large ſpoonfuls of fine flour, and a little ſalt, for quarter of an hour, put to them one quart and a half of milk, mix them well together, then butter a dripping pan and ſet it under beef, mutton or a loin of veal when roaſting, and when it is brown, cut it in ſquare pieces and turn it over, when well browned ſend it to the table on a diſh.

The meat would be roast on a spit or Dutch oven.
Older dalesfolk remember puddings being turned over in this way.

39

Bread had mainly been baked in communal ovens until the wooden houses were gradually replaced by stone in the 17th and 18th centuries. Even then, to avoid risk of fire the bake house was often a separate building close to the main house. There was a wide fireplace with smoke hood above, then built into the wall beside it a brick-lined beehive-shaped bread oven, closed by a small iron door. On baking day sticks were burnt inside this until the required heat was achieved. Then the embers were raked out, the bricks cleaned and the loaves put in. Full use was made of the gradually lessening heat of the oven to cook pies and cakes and finally to dry the kindling for the next firing.

Only half the bread oven at West End House remains, the rest having been destroyed when it was walled up, but it gives us a good view of the interior. (Lower drawing shows a cross-section view of a complete oven.) The archway over the top is a puzzle, perhaps to take the weight of the wall above?

To Make a Sauce for a Green Goose (1741)

Take the juice of Sorrel, a little butter, and a few scalded gooseberries, mix them together and sweeten it to your Taste; you must not let it boil after you put in the Sorrel, if you do it will take off the Green. You must put this sauce into a Bason.

Think of the poor cook pounding away to make sorrel juice! Now we can whizz a few leaves in a liquidiser, add the (cooled) lightly stewed gooseberries, butter and sugar and it's done in a couple of minutes. Don't wait until you next have goose, it makes a piquant and colourful sauce to serve cold with smoked mackerel or sliced chicken.

To Make a Goose Pye

Take two geese at Christmas, cut them down the backs, and take out all the bones, season them well with mace and pepper, salt and nutmeg; wrap one within the other, and raise a crust that will just hold them, lay them in, run the knife point into the skin in several places to prevent them rising; put butter over and lid it, and when baked pour in clarified butter. This is real goose pye

Ann Pickham of Leeds in 1773

Goose pies were made on St Stephen's day, December 26th, and shared amongst the needy in the neighbourhood.

Around 1790 Geese from Dent, Sedbergh, Garsdale, Swaledale, Mallerstang and Wensleydale were driven by dealers to Richmond and Darlington, Lancashire and West Riding. Flocks of about 1,000

walked 7 miles a day starting at 4am until 6 pm, walking for half a mile, resting for half a mile. They were driven through hot tar and then sand, to strengthen their feet.

Yorkshire Christmas Pie

First make a good standing crust, let the wall be very thick: bone a turkey, a goose, a fowl, a partridge and a pigeon; season them all very well, take half an ounce of mace, half an ounce of nutmegs, a quarter of an ounce of cloves, and half an ounce of black pepper, all beat fine together, two large spoonsful of salt, and then mix them together, open the fowls all down the back, and bone them; first the pigeon, then the partridge; cover them; then the fowl, then the goose, and then the turkey, which must be large; season them all well first, and lay them in the crust, so as it will look only like a whole turkey; then have a hare ready cased and wiped with a clean cloth; cut it into pieces, that is, joint it; season it, and lay it as close as you can get on one side; on the other side woodcocks, moor game, and what sort of wild fowl you can get; season them well and lay them close; put at least four pounds of butter into the pie, then lay on your lid, which must be a very thick one, and let it be well baked; it must have a very hot oven, and it will take at least four hours.

This crust will take a bushel of flour. These pies are often sent to London in a box, as presents; therefore the walls must be well built.

from Hannah Glasse in 1796

Chickens boiled with Bacon and Celery

Boil two chickens very white in a pot by themſelves, and a piece of ham, or good thick bacon; boil two bunches of celery tender; then cut them about two inches long, all the white part; put it into a ſaucepan, with half a pint of cream, a piece of butter rolled in flour, and ſome pepper and ſalt; ſet it on the fire and ſhake it often: when it is thick and fine, lay your chickens in the diſh, and pour your ſauce in the middle, that the celery may lie between the fowls; and garniſh the diſh all round with ſlices of ham or bacon.

N.B. If you have cold ham in the houſe, that, cut into ſlices and broiled, does full as well, or better, to lay round the diſh.

Hannah Glasse

TO STEW PARSNIPS

Boil them tender, ſcrape them from the duſt, cut them into ſlices, put them into a ſauce-pan with cream enough; for ſauce, a piece of butter rolled in flour, a little ſalt, and ſhake the ſaucepan often; when the cream boils, pour them into a plate for a corner diſh, or a ſide diſh at ſupper.

TO MAKE A HODGE-PODGE

Take a piece of beef, fat and lean together, about a pound of veal, a pound of ſcrag of mutton, cut all into little pieces, ſet it on the fire, with two quarts of water, an ounce of barley, an onion, a little bundle of ſweet herbs, three or four heads of celery waſhed clean and cut ſmall, a little mace, two or three cloves ſome whole pepper, tied all in a muſlin rag, and put to the meat three turnips pared and cut in two, a large carrot ſcraped clean and cut in ſix pieces, a little lettuce cut ſmall, put it all in the pot and cover it cloſe: let it ſtew very softly over a ſlow fire five or ſix hours; take out the ſpice, ſweet herbs and onion, and pour all into a ſoup diſh, and ſend it to table; firſt ſeaſon it with ſalt. Half a pint of green peas, when it is the ſeaſon for them, is very good. If you let this boil faſt, it will waſte too much; therefore you cannot do it too ſlow, if it does but ſimmer.

TO MAKE A KARRAT PUDDING

Take a quart of cream & half a pint of milk & ſeven eggs keep out 3 of ye whites take 3 or 4 karrats clenſed and waſhed & great ym then take the quantity of half a peney loaf greated also mix all this together in a pan & ſtur it well put in ſuger ſalt & Nutmeg to your taſte when it goes in ye oven you muſt melt almoſt a quarter of a Pound of freſh butter & ſtur it in ye pudding you may put in ſweetmeats and candied Oring Lemons & ſitten pills morry will do very well to ſtick on ye pudding when it goes into ye Oven you may take ye 3 Whites ye keept out of ye pudding & make a thin puff paſte wth a little Sugar in it to line ye diſh you bake it in you must put in ye Buttor & sweetmeats just as it goes in ye Oven & ſtur it or elce ye ſweetmeats will ſink to ye bottom one hour will beak ym.

sitten pills = citron peels! A penny loaf weighed about 8 oz.

This 19th century excerpt from the local paper shows that nostalgia for the 'good old days' is no new thing.:

The Wensleydale Advertiser of 24th December 1844 -
"CHRISTMAS CUSTOMS ....These ancient customs, remnants of the merry days of old, are more generally practised amongst the valleys of the Northern parts of Yorkshire and of Westmorland and Cumberland, over which the ever-changing tide of fashion has not yet swept, than in any other parts of England...... On these happy festive occasions do not let the customs and enjoyments of our fore-elders, and of our youthful days be forgotten, for they will revive in us many pleasing associations, many delightful recollections...... Let a store of the old-fashioned Yule cakes duly prepared with spices and condiments appear at the tea-table.."
"We have run after the Bishopdale hounds and tested of the

hospitality of the members of the hunt - we have followed the Middleham Harriers at this season - St Stevens day of course - with a share of Christmas cake in one pocket and of Yule in the other........"
There are recipes for Yule Cakes in the Traditional section.

There was much overcrowding and poverty in the villages. Those who could no longer survive ended up in workhouses such as Bainbridge, where life was harsh but where they probably fared better than before - Marie Hartley and Joan Ingilby give a graphic account of the meals there in *'Yorkshire Village'*

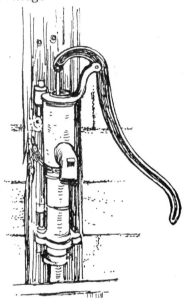

"On forms drawn up to long tables set with mess tins, knives, forks, spoons and pewter plates, they sat down to breakfasts of gulls (porridge) and milk, and occasionally treacle, washed down with either coffee or beer, and to meagre dinners that early in the century consisted of broth, pease soup, bread and cheese. But by the forties and sixties the midday meal had improved, and most days either beast head, mutton hash, beef, potatoes or fried onions appeared on the menu, and sometimes 'berry pie'. Supper remained a dull meal - 'whay sops,' milk, and oatmeal, or tea and bread and butter."

The 19th century saw the revival of non-conformist religious fervour, and with it the battle against the "demon drink". In the period from 1830 to 1880 chapel Love Feasts were held, when on a diet of bread, biscuits or fruit loaf and a large communal cup of water
".....the whole atmosphere could become charged with a dynamic emotional force, the affecting cries of the penitents being lost amid the bursting joy of triumphant faith".
Tea festivals were held on Leyburn Shawl when up to 3,000 people were present. *(Imagine the organisation and the baking involved!)* Every chapel also had its annual Tea Party.

45

In this same period numerous dalesfolk left for the cotton mills of Lancashire.   Others went to Liverpool where some ran milk houses. Hundreds emigrated to America, many of whom had eked out a meagre living in farming by working in the then declining leadmines.   Wisconsin attracted them because it had both good farmlands and a lead-mining industry.

The following extracts are from a collection of letters and Dinsdale/Chapman family history published privately in the U.S.A. by Abigail Curkeet as "The Circuit Rider" (The Dales Countryside Museum has a copy).

It is apparent from this first letter that the traditional high tea followed by a cooked supper later in the evening was regarded as essential in Wensleydale.   The Dinsdales had a small farm and a grocery shop in Askrigg, but times were hard and there are many references to poor prices obtained for stock, cheese and butter.

Elizabeth Dinsdale writing from Askrigg to her son Matthew in Wisconsin in 1845:

"Matthew Willis letter has set the pepel all of talking hear, he says you have no Tea but green and milk is scarce and Butter and Cheese he has seen none and you only get three meals a Day and you say you have all you want I fear you make the Best of it my Dear Matthew."

Matthew's letter to his brother remarks on "mother's list of woes"
"We only have three meals a day, I thought she knew that long ago. But I will tell her something new. Many families have

46

only two. This is not because the people have not the provisions, but because they do not want to be always cooking and eating. I eat three times a day and I should be very sorry if I had to eat oftener".

1845   Letter from Matthew Dinsdale to advise would-be emigrants on provisions for the journey to America.

"Employ the ship's cook, he will be worth what he may charge; all has to be prepared by him and he bakes roasts or boils as the case may be.. They must have provisions for six weeks, they can calculate how much will be sufficient for each person. Ham or bacon, plenty of potatoes which you may purchase at Liverpool, flour, some oat meal biscuits which make good pudding when soaked in water for a few hours. Get the best, do not bake anything at home for the sea except it be oat bread, cheese, butter, eggs which keep very well in flour. Preserves, pickles, vinegar, best French brandy for medicine, arrow root, carbonate of soda and acid tartar, sugar, tea, coffee, salt, rice, raisins, currants, fish (salt herring), peas for soup, candles and a lanthern. If you can make yeast on ship-board and make cakes that would be first rate"

When Matthew's brother John, his wife Tirzah and family went out to America in 1849 they found they had to throw overboard the boiled hung meat they had taken., but they mention that their bread was well-baked by the ships cook. (*Hung meat was pickled beef.*)

In 1850 sister Elizabeth writes from Askrigg:
"We were singing at Thoralby Tea Party last week and got great praise, we think we can do as well as the Swaledale singers we have practised a good deal lately."
These excerpts from brother Edward's contribution to the same letter give a picture of their chapel-dominated social life:
"Tuesday evening I am now sitting by our own fireside my Mother only beside myself. Elizabeth has gone to Carperby to the Sunday school Tea festival. Mr and Mrs Morton are with her they are all who are going from Askrigg. We had our festival as usual on New Years day we had not so large a company as we sometimes have had - how it happened we cannot tell but it was a pleasant day. We had a preacher from Liverpool......
....According to old custom we had our Tea the day after and then

47

the Yearly Meeting....... We had the singers out of Swaledale but we are quite tired of them. They do not Sing so well as they used to and another thing their conduct is very unbecoming they are too fond of their glass we have felt very much this Year they went to the Inn and staid up till 3 o'clock in the Morning and then next day they went to Carperby to sing and got almost drunk.........

"This is my birthday I am 28 years old...........This morning we had Judge Marshall and James Robinson to breakfast - to dinner we had Mrs Morten and James Little and to Tea we had Mrs Morten and Mary Blades and to supper we had in addition Mr Morten and Matthew Thompson. You see on my birthday we keep up quite a feast, it was not designed it just happened so. Judge Marshall is a Teetotal Lecturer from America he gives his lectures Free of charge.........

But I must tell you how it happened our other visitors came to be here. Elizabeth is making me some shirts and the above named Ladies came to help her and the two gentlemen dropped in in a friendly way."

(How I wish he had mentioned what they ate!)

This excerpt from Gayle Dexter Hughes' childhood memories of John Dinsdale in "The Circuit Rider" shows that some local recipes went to Wisconsin with the emigrants.

"Grandpa always helped with the milking, which was important on that farm. He always wore a long coat with a belt round his waist and carried a stool in his hand. There was a creamery in Preston *(named after Matthew Preston, also from Askrigg)*, less than a mile away, to which the milk was taken. Later came the cheese factory. Oh how delicious were the big daisy cheeses which came from there. And then there were other goodies. Aunt Libbie would get curd cheese from the cheese factory with which she made the most savoury cheesecakes. How we did enjoy them!

Grandpa was very fond of many English dishes such as Cornish pasties, Yorkshire pudding, English currant cookies, and mutton *(surely pork?)* with apple sauce."

I have not yet found out whether the recipe for cheesecakes made by Aunt Libbie (who left Askrigg as a baby) has survived amongst any of John and Tirzah's 600 or so descendants, but THE HUNT IS ON.....

Cheesecakes were traditionally made in Swaledale on the Fridays before Whitsuntide and Midsummer festivities, and eaten with the joint of beef instead of the usual bread. *(So says Peter Brears in "Traditional Food in Yorkshire". They must have been somewhat plainer than the ones we know!)*

Muker's "Aud Roy" celebrations on 6th January began with a group of local lads wearing large aprons. They held these out to collect offerings from the women, who threw cheesecakes, Yule cakes and cooked meats for the communal celebration. In Wensleydale the Redmire Cheesecake Gatherers had baskets, wore fancy dress and blackened their faces when collecting for Redmire Feast (a tradition which continued up to 1910).

Methods of preserving food for the winter had changed little over the years. Meat fish and vegetables were salted, smoked, potted or dried, fruits made into jams, jellies and wines.

Preserving eggs. A recipe of 1878 - Pour 2 gallons of water boiling hot on to 2 quarts of quick lime & 25 lbs of salt. When quite cold mix into it 1oz Cream of Tartar. The following day put the eggs in.
(My mother used to 'put them down' in isinglass. When I was about two she caught me lifting them out one by one and dropping them back into the enamel pail ......)

Janet Rawlins

49

Alexander Tiplady fought at the battle of Waterloo, then came home to Wensleydale to open a shop in Bainbridge. He was a grocer and also a hosier, *(A hosier was an agent who collected the hand-knitted stockings for which the dale was famous, and sold them on.)*

His great grand-daughter Edith Leyland recounts her memories of this same village shop:

"I was born in 1899, so that the village shop I remember was very different from the one I know now in 1993. One big difference is in opening times. I remember when we opened our shop at 8 a.m and closed at 9 p.m. (10 p.m. on Saturdays). When I retired in 1963 the times were 8.30 to 6.0, now the shop is self-service and opens 9 a.m. and closes at 5.30 p.m.

"Most groceries are pre-wrapped now. In my day we weighed and packed sugar, lard, flour, yeast, tea, rice etc, ground coffee as needed with an ancient grinder, made our own baking powder, blended our own tea (to suit the local water), cleaned the dried fruit. We drew vinegar from a small wooden barrel, treacle from another. Customers often brought their own containers. I don't know when margarine appeared, but it came in blocks in wooden boxes and we had to cut and weigh and pack that. Biscuits came 'loose' in big boxes and we had to weigh those too. The brass scales with their row of weights had to be polished each week, as had the big mahogany counter. There were strong blue paper bags for sugar, cream ones for other goods. For smaller quantities we twisted a sheet of paper into a poke (a cone), folding down the top to seal it and it was a matter of pride to make a neat parcel..

"We sold only one variety of cheese, Wensleydale. My father

(and later, my brother) was also a cheese factor, and sold wholesale chiefly in the North East. After summer he went to farms to test cheese and then went north for orders. We had a cheese warehouse with shelves on three sides and full at the busy season. Each cheese was turned over on alternate days. Later these were sent away by train and sometimes we children helped to mark each cheese with an initial in black ink. Every tenth one had an addressed label tacked on the top.

We passed these cheeses from hand to hand to the driver to put in the cart - no boxes or cartons - but of course the cheeses were very firm and bound with calico. I don't know what happened at the station!

"We sold many things, I don't know what to mention next. We sold soap in long bars and cut them up too, as customers wished. Large blocks of salt and also salt-petre for bacon curing. Paraffin, linseed oil, red 'rudd' and blue paste for marking sheep, fire bricks, petrol (after the 1914-18 war) - Pratt's, in 2 gallon green tins. We needed it for our motor transport, an ancient Austin runabout which we called Jane. All those smelly things we kept in the "cooper's shop" - a lean-to at the end of the house; presumably there was a cooper in the village at one time.

(Illustration- Tea urn given to Edith's mother Mary Tiplady on her marriage)

"I think it would be about 1918 when my father bought Aaron Knagg's business. This was a chemist and druggist. There were various veterinary medicines, I remember "red drench". There was a small phial of mercury, my brother and I used to empty this into a saucer and swish it about. It made pretty little balls which fascinated us. We sold other patent medicines... I can't start on that list! I do remember that an elderly gent used to come to our back door early in the morning with a tea-cup, with a request for sixpennyworth of nitre. I think it was used as a medicine for lambs...he needed it for 'the morning after the night before'!

"When I left Ackworth school I went to Keighley to learn millinery. Then owing to my father's illness I returned home to help in the shop, and occasionally would make and trim hats. Upstairs we had a drapery showroom where we had men's and women's underwear; health flannel; hessian in 2 widths for stobbed rugs (later it had designs printed on); cheese calico; butter muslin; ribbons; lace and hats. My mother and I would go to Bradford to buy 'fents' which were sold by weight, then bring them home and weigh out the various remnants of velvet, wool and other fabrics.

"In 1929 we took over Johnsons greengrocery business and moved over the road to the present shop. About this time bread and cakes started to be delivered from Skipton.

Many customers expected credit, and a number were 'reluctant' to settle their accounts. One particular mother would send her little boy to the shop - I remember an occasion when he came for tinned salmon and biscuits. Knowing we would be unlikely to be paid for a long time, if at all, I sent the lower quality salmon and plain biscuits. A few minutes later he was back 'Me mum says she wants red salmon, and chocolate biscuits'."

Bainbridge in the twenties was pretty self-sufficient. Flour and oatmeal could be bought from the corn merchant, there was a hardware shop, two grocers, a greengrocer, a bakery, a butcher, a post office newsagent and sweet shop.

Mary Bell, known to all as Gill Gate Mary, was born at Gill Gate on Low Abbotside, married a local farmer and has lived there all her life. Here are her reminiscences of Pig Killing and Haytime, which illustrate just what was expected of a Dales cook.

PIG KILLING

"In the days before we had deep-freezes pig killing kept a housewife and helpers busy for most of the week. The day the pig was killed the blood had to be dealt with immediately. It had to be stirred continually until it was cold, to stop it from curdling, then made into black puddings and baked in the oven for several hours. After the pig had hung for 24 hours it was cut up and salted, except for the fat, which was pulled from the sides of the pig's ribs. This fat was cut up in small pieces and rendered down, the fat poured off and stored in jars for use in making pastry during the year.

"The bits of skinny fat that remained were called crappins and eaten cold with salt and bread. As a rule there would be too many crappins for one family so they would be shared out with friends and neighbours. The liver, backbone (chine) spare rib and lean pork cuttings were also shared. The lean pork cuttings were cooked for several hours in pie dishes. When cold the fat which formed over the top kept the meat sealed, it would keep for several weeks and could then be made into pork pies.

"The head and legs were salted and after a period of time were made into brawn with stewing beef added. Sausages could be made too, but required a sausage machine. The sides and hams (back legs) were left in salt for 3 weeks, then taken out and hung in the farmhouse kitchen to dry. The bacon lasted a household about a year.

HAYTIME

"Haytime has changed over the years although the method in the Dales follows the same pattern. Haymaking used to start the first or second week in July when the Irishmen came to Hawes for the haytime hirings. Since the arrival of the tractor the social and friendly nature of haymaking has disappeared, it is no longer safe for children to help and play around.

"In pre-tractor days the cutting of the grass had to be done early in the morning, perhaps as early as 4am, because later it would be too hot for the horses to work. Mowing was very hard work, epecially on the dales hillsides.

"Breakfast taken out to the field consisted of fried bacon and egg sandwiches, marmalade sandwiches and a can of hot tea. There would be the man mowing, a boy or girl raking the grass away from the unmown grass to make it easier for the mower, and a man, probably Irish, mowing with a scythe around the walls and steeper parts.

"About 10am another snack would be taken along to the field. By this time the rest of the haytimers would be working, getting the grass turned over and dried ready for hay if the day was fine and sunny. This 'drinkings' usually consisted of bread and cheese with scones or bannocks or biscuits, with hot coffee to drink.

"Twelve o'clock was dinner time when everybody including the horses came home for a good feed, unless the fields were a mile or so away from the farmhouse, then it meant more sandwiches and packing up of food. This was the main meal of the day and consisted of a roast or good stew and a pudding.

"Four o'clock, time for tea, which was carried out in baskets. This consisted of some kind of sandwiches - lettuce, tomato, banana, egg, tinned fish, or potted meat. Scones, teacake, fruit pies made of apple, gooseberries, blackcurrant, raspberries or rhubarb. Then fruit cake, biscuits and buns. By this hour of the day the hay was usually being gathered into the barn either by horse and sledge or a hay sweep, with a boy or girl riding on the horse. In poor weather when it was difficult to get the hay dry it was made into huts or pikes. These were large mounds of hay which stood for a few days before being taken to the barn or shed.

"At tea time several extra helpers had often gathered up and came to partake of the tea basket. Sometimes their children too came to play in the hayfield and enjoy the contents of the basket. Carrying food, mugs and a huge can of hot tea for about twenty people, and sometimes pushing a child in a pram as well, was no easy task! After tea some of the men would do the milking while the rest got on with the hay. Seven o'clock was time for another break when the basket was packed again with meat sandwiches or meat pies, scones, cakes and coffee to drink. The haymaking usually continued until about nine o'clock, struggling against the midges!

"In the days when horses were used there was a great deal of hand raking to be done to make it easier for the machines to cut the hay. The majority of farmers would get horse-drawn machinery during the first world war, and tractors came to the Dales during the second world war.

"When the work was finished for the day all the workers came home for supper. This consisted of cold meat and salad, or pies, or perhaps a 'fryup', or ham and eggs.

"The farmer's wife and any help she might have in the house were expected to go into the hayfield to help. In their spare moments (!!) they had to bake the bread, pastry and cakes, cook the meats, clean the house, do the washing and the shopping, wash the milk cans night and morning, feed the hens, look after the children, and make lemonade and ginger beer to bottle and take out to the field. On wet days she was able to catch up with the housework. She did not have many rest days except for Sunday.

"Haymaking was not done on a Sunday until the second world war. It made an agreeable change to be able to go out in the sunshine and work in the hayfield, we were able to talk and discuss what our neighbours were doing at the other side of the valley. Now people cannot hear themselves speak for the noise of the tractors.

When we had a good summer haytime lasted about three weeks. In wet summers it could be as late as October before the hay was in. In 1992 the hay was made in one week."

SECTION II
TRADITIONAL DALES FOOD

I have to thank the people who lent me old family recipe books for this section, which conjure up pictures of huge baking days, farmhouse tables laden with pastries and scones and cakes. In the early part of this century cholesterol was unheard of, and hard physical work burned off the calories!

The famous Yorkshire high tea is still in favour although perhaps not in its former magnificence. A five o'clock meal suits a lot of people - in many Dales homes a cooked supper follows as well.

There are comparatively few references to the cooking of meat dishes in the old cookbooks, there was I suppose no need to write down instructions as opposed to recipes. Oven temperatures varied so much and each cook knew her own. They had to adapt from the old cast iron range, to paraffin stoves (during the coal strike in the 20's), and then to electric cookers, solid fuel or calor gas stoves. Certainly a great deal of meat was eaten. There were three butcher's shops in Askrigg in the 1930s, now there are none.

Salads, and fresh vegetables too, rarely merit a mention except in methods of preserving, but most people had their vegetable patch and fruit trees. There have been markets for hundreds of years and there were greengrocer's shops as early as the 18th century.

Recipes for puddings and cakes (baking as opposed to cooking) were passed around and the same ones crop up in various parts of the dales. There are numerous steamed puddings, some needing 5 or 6 hours cooking time (little wonder that we rarely cook them now except at Christmas - few of us spend so long in or near the kitchen). I wondered about all that steam filling the house thereby showing my ignorance of the kitchen range, when the steam would go up the chimney.

Some of the old cookbooks contain reminders of the shortages in the second world war. One recipe was for 'War butter', where a pint of milk, a tablespoon of gelatine and a dessert spoon of salt was added to 1 lb butter to make 2 lbs. 'Wartime marmalade' had lemon substitute; there was an eggless Welsh rarebit; dried egg was used in various recipes; 'almond paste' was made with almond essence and soya flour, and the Christmas pudding contained potatoes as well as the familiar carrot.

I have not given metric quantities in this section as they seemed inappropriate with the old-time recipes. (I should mention that the Yorkshire gill measures half a pint, not a quarter of a pint as in other parts of the country). There is a chart at the back of the book giving weights and measures.

First from Marie Hartley and Joan Ingilby, Founder-Presidents of the Friends of the Dales Countryside Museum.

Joan Ingilby's SHAPE   (Cornflour Mould)

1 oz cornflour	1 egg
1 pt milk (rather more)	pinch salt
1 oz butter	1 oz caster sugar

flavouring - very little vanilla essence

Put milk and flavouring in a pan and allow to become hot.   Blend the flour with a little cold milk. Strain the hot milk over, and add beaten egg, salt and sugar. Return to pan and stir till boiling. Add butter. Turn into a wetted mould and when set turn out.   Delicious served with stewed raspberries or any fruit and a little cream.

Marie Hartley's YORKSHIRE PUDDING

1 egg	3 oz flour
½ pt milk	1 teasp salt

(Miss Hartley keeps an 8 in. square tin specially for Yorkshire pudding and never uses small bun tins!)
Briskly whisk the egg in a good-sized basin, add a little milk, work in the flour, beat well with a spoon with holes in it. Add the rest of the milk. The consistency is thin.   Leave for at least one hour. Heat in the tin a knob of fat to blue heat, and pour in the mixture.   Bake at 450º F for about half an hour.   Serve with gravy (and sometimes mint sauce) and eat as a first course, by itself. Also delicious with raspberry vinegar.

RASPBERRY VINEGAR

1 lb of raspberries   **1 pt malt vinegar**

Put raspberries and vinegar in a bowl and leave for 2 days, stirring occasionally.   Then strain (squeeze the pulp if you wish but the liquid will then be slightly cloudy).   Add just short of a pound of sugar to each pint of juice.   Bring slowly to the boil then boil for 20 minutes. Bottle when cool.

YORKSHIRE PUDDING AND POTATOES   (Mary Wrigley)

Make a **Yorkshire Pudding batter** and season with **salt and pepper** , some **sage** and a little **onion** chopped finely.   Now add some **cooked potatoes** and bake like any other Yorkshire Pudding and if you can manage it put some **bacon** on the top after you have turned it. *(Turning - see section I)*

A tip from Margaret Hopper.
When making Yorkshire pudding, before pouring into the tin add a dash of the coldest water you can find - preferably snow!

A century-old recipe from **Margaret Hopper** for

CHEESE PUDDING

3 oz rich grated cheese	**½ teasp dry mustard**
2 oz fine breadcrumbs	**salt, pepper**
a grain of cayenne	**1 small cupful milk**
1 oz melted butter	**1 well-beaten egg**

Beat all well together for 10 minutes and bake in a moderate oven. Serve on hot buttered toast.

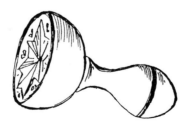

OATCAKE

This could be in either this section or the previous one, the local names of **HAVERCAKE** or **HAVERBREAD**, made from Havermeal giving the clue to its historic origins, for it comes from the Old Norse *hafri,* meaning oats.

Marie Hartley and Joan Ingilby have thoroughly researched the making and baking of the various types for their book *'Life and Tradition in the Yorkshire Dales'* which includes a fascinating chapter on the subject.

There are two kinds of oatcake; one made from a batter which produces a long oval, soft cake *(which I remember buying in Leeds market and eating buttered, spread with syrup and rolled up),* and the kind made in the northern dales which is rolled out, baked on a backstone and then dried.

The earliest backstones were flat oval stones which would be heated in a fire. Then in the western dales many farms had them built-in with a fire-box beneath (later the stones were superseded by iron). However the northern dales used a portable round iron griddle-type backstone.

When dried, the havercake (or haverbread) would keep for a long time.

It seems to me they are due for a revival in preference to the expensive packaged oatcakes from Scotland, especially with today's emphasis on a high fibre diet!

HAVERCAKE (OATCAKE)
(Mary Halton)

1½ cups oatmeal
1 cup flour
a walnut of lard
salt

Mix together and add cold water to a stiff paste. Roll out and bake in a moderate oven. If to keep they should be dried by the fire on an easel.

61

CLAP CAKE (a type of Oatcake)   (Isobel Leyland)

1 lb oatmeal	½ lb flour
½ teasp carb. soda	1 teasp baking powder
4 oz lard	salt

Mix with milk. Roll out and cut into squares then triangles.

My Mother's SAVOURY PUDDING

2 large onions	3 oz suet
1 egg, beaten	2 tablesp oatmeal
½ oz dripping	salt and pepper
8 oz stale bread, both white and brown	
1 dessertsp dried herbs	

Slice onions and boil. Slice bread thickly and cut into chunks, soak in the water in which onions were boiled. Drain bread but do not squeeze dry. *(On the other hand, my mother-in-law's recipe says squeeze the bread very dry!)* Add oatmeal, grated suet, egg, herbs and seasoning and mix. Pre-heat a baking tin with half oz dripping until sizzling, spread mixture about half inch thick. Bake in a fairly hot oven about 1 hour until crisp and brown on top.
Delicious with pork or turkey, or make a vegetarian version with vegetarian 'suet'

MEAT LOAF, or filling for MEAT PIE   from Peg Scarr
(Coleby Hall) who made it each year after pig-killing.

1¾ lbs pork
4 oz bacon
2 eggs
4 oz breadcrumbs
1 cooking apple, grated
salt, pepper & parsley
a little minced onion

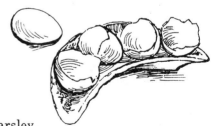

Mince pork & bacon. Chop parsley. Mix all well together, and if making meat loaf line tin with **streaky bacon.** Bake 45 mins.

SALMON MOULD

A popular Sunday tea-time treat just after the war when tinned salmon was still in short supply. My mother's version was uncooked. She mashed a **tin of pink salmon**, added a drop of **cochineal** (to pretend it was red salmon!) **breadcrumbs** and a splash of **malt vinegar.** This was pressed into a shallow dish and covered with a **fairly thick white sauce.** When cool this was covered with alternating stripes of **hard boiled egg yolk, finely chopped whites sprinkled with cayenne or paprika pepper, and chopped parsley.**

AUNTIE CALVERT'S SALMON MOULD
(Elizabeth Metcalfe)

1 tin of salmon
1 dessertsp chopped parsley
1 oz butter
a little lemon juice

2 oz breadcrumbs

1 egg
salt and pepper

Take the salmon, clean all the skin and bone away. Add breadcrumbs, butter (melted) and chopped parsley to taste, a squeeze of lemon juice, salt and pepper and 1 egg to bind together. Steam for 20 mins. Serve either hot or cold.

RABBIT CAKE
(Mary Bell)

2 rabbits
1 onion, chopped
parsley
2 eggs
milk

1 slice of ham
1 slice of bread
pepper and salt
2 oz butter, melted

Take the meat off 2 boiled rabbits. Put through the mincing machine with the ham. Soak the bread in some milk, mix in a basin with onion, parsley, 2 beaten eggs, salt & pepper and the melted butter. Add minced meat, mix well together, press into a mould and bake for 1 hour. Serve cold.

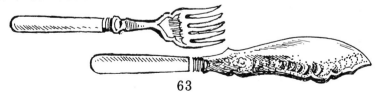

JUGGED HARE   (Elma Banks)
Seasonable from September to end of February

1 hare cut into neat pieces
2 oz bacon fat
A few thin slices of bacon
6 peppercorns
2 large onions
each stuck with 2 cloves
rind of half a lemon
pinch cayenne pepper
1 blade mace
bunch of sweet herbs
salt and pepper
2 pts water
½ pt port

Divide hare into neat joints, saving as much of the blood as possible. Fry joints briskly in bacon fat until they are a good brown colour. Lay the bacon slices in a deep earthenware jug (heavy stew pot) then put in the hare pieces, the onions, lemon rind, peppercorns, cayenne pepper, mace, herbs, seasoning and water. Cover with tightly fitting lid and bake in a fairly slow oven for two hours or until the hare is tender. Pour the gravy through a sieve into a pan. Remove spices, rind and herbs and keep meat warm.   Work 2 oz butter on a plate with a palette knife until soft and knead in 2 oz flour a little at a time to form a smooth paste. Reheat the gravy and thicken with the butter and flour.   Add half a pint of port wine and one tablesp redcurrant jelly and simmer gently until jelly has dissolved. Blend a little of the gravy with the blood of the hare and add to the rest.   Do not reboil. Adjust seasoning, strain gravy over the hare. Serve with more redcurrant jelly and forcemeat balls.

POTTED PIGEON   (Elma Banks)

3 pigeons   salt and pepper
melted butter   Worcestershire sauce

Skin and clean the pigeons.   Place them in a pan, cover with water and boil until the meat is leaving the bones. Remove from fire and, when cool enough to handle, carefully take away all the bones. Mince the meat finely.   Put the bones back into the saucepan and boil until the water has reduced to about a cupful.   Season and add

64

a dash of Worcester sauce if liked. Moisten with stock from bones and a little melted butter. Press into jars and run a little melted butter on tops.

ROLLED STEAK (Alice Chapman)

Take **1 lb lean steak**, beat it with a rolling pin to make it tender, make a **sage and onion stuffing** and spread the stuffing over one side of the steak. Roll up and tie with string. Put some dripping into a roasting tin and roast the steak for one hour, frequently basting it. (Boil the onions partly before making the stuffing).

EGG AND BACON PIE (Mary Bell)

8 oz flour	2 oz lard
2 oz margarine	8 teasp cold water
8 oz cooked shoulder or ham	salt & pepper

Mix flour and salt and rub in fat. Make into a stiff paste by adding water. Divide pastry into two and roll out. Line 8" pie plate. Cut ham into small pieces and add to 3 beaten eggs. Pour mixture onto prepared plate and cover with second round. Make a small hole in the top and brush over with milk and egg. Bake in moderate hot oven, 35 to 40 mins.

BEEF OLIVES (Mrs Blythe, Hardrow)

4 oz fat raw ham	1 apple
1 lb steak	1 teasp thyme
1 onion	1 tablesp flour
4 oz breadcrumbs	pepper & salt
1 dessertsp parsley	

Cut meat into strips about 3" long by 2" wide, put a little stuffing on each, roll up and tie with string, dredge each with flour thickly, melt about 2 oz dripping or fat ham in a frying pan and fry olives until brown on both sides, lift out into stew jar, add half oz flour to fat in pan, mix thoroughly, add slowly half pt warm liquid, stir until boiling and pour over meat, cover and stew in oven 1 hour, or very slowly for 2 hours.

CARROT PUDDING

8 oz flour   8 oz potatoes
8 oz carrots   4 oz suet
8 oz currants   8 oz raisins
2 oz candied peel   4 oz treacle
2 oz sliced almonds

No instructions for this unusual recipe - original quantities were for four times this quantity, and 'boil 6 hours'.

FIG PUDDING

12 oz bread, grated   8 oz best figs
6 oz suet   6 oz moist sugar
teacupful of milk   nutmeg
1 egg

The figs and suet must be chopped very fine. Mix the bread and suet first, then the figs and sugar and nutmeg, and egg well beaten, and then the milk. Boil in a mould 4 hours. To be eaten with sweet sauce.

CRUMPLY PUDDING

1 qt milk   4 tablesp flour
2 eggs   4 oz moist sugar
1 teacup finely chopped suet
candied lemon or
orange peel, raisins, or preserved ginger, chopped

Grease a mould, stick it all over with raisins and peel or ginger. Make the flour into a smooth paste with the milk. Add the eggs and sugar. Pour this into the mould, place sufficient suet on the top to cover it all over. Bake in a moderate oven until the suet looks brown and set. Turn out and serve very hot.

BEAR PARK PUDDING (Catherine Willis)

This is her Grandmother's recipe from Bear Park, where Hilda Shannon was cook for years and years and always produced it as a treat. (Everyone loved it...except Catherine!) When C. married Theo Willis from Manor House, Carperby his mother also made it but called it Scalded Flour pudding. However the Bear Park Pudding which appears in a Bainbridge cook's book is the same in principle but does not separate the eggs. One wonders if Hilda Shannon was hanging on to the secret of folding in the beaten whites!

2 tablesp flour	2 tablesp sugar
1 oz butter	1 pt milk
2 eggs	
lemon rind, or chocolate	

Mix together smoothly flour, sugar and butter.   Add boiling milk, stirring all the time.   Add flavouring.   When nearly cold mix in beaten yolks and fold in stiffly beaten whites.   Pour into a grand dish and bake 30 mins in mod. oven.

AUNTIE NELLIE'S SHERRY FLUFF

Whip **half pt cream** until very thick.   Still whipping, add the strained juice of **a small orange,**
2 level tablesp caster sugar   3 tablesp dark sherry
Put in a cold place until the next day.   By then the mixture will have separated into golden liquid and pale fluff.

NORWEGIAN SOUFFLÉ (Peg Scarr)
This recipe comes from her grandmother Peggy Storey who was cook to Lord Bolton in the latter part of the 19th Century

3 eggs, separated	½ cup caster sugar
1 glass sherry	½ oz gelatine
¼ pt hot water	

Beat egg yolks and sugar well together.   Melt gelatine in the water. Whisk whites until stiff.   Mix all together, pour into bowl and leave to set, then cover with raspberry jam and cream.

APPLE COBS (Mary Wrigley)

6 oz brown sugar, 3 apples, 6 oz shortcrust pastry
Peel and core apples. Put the pastry on a well-floured board, place the apple in the centre and work the pastry round with the tips of the fingers, till almost closed up. Fill up the core with brown sugar, sprinkle more on the pastry, wet the edges and carefully close the pastry over the sugar. Roll on the floured board until quite round. Place with the joined side down and bake in a fairly hot oven, 20 to 30 mins according to the size of the apples.

HAYTIME (see Mary Bell's reminiscences of the vast quantities of food taken out to the fields!)
HAYTIME CAKE (Mary Bell)

2 lbs flour	salt	1 lb currants
1 lb sugar		1 lb raisins
12 oz margarine		4 oz peel
2 dessertsp vinegar		2 teasp carb soda
pinch of mixed spice		milk

Rub marge into flour, then add sugar, fruit and spice. Mix vinegar, carb soda and milk and add to dry ingredients. Mix well. Put into greased loaf tins, stand for 2 hours then bake for 3 hours in a moderate oven.

HAYTIME DRINK - GINGER BEER (Elma Banks)

2½ lbs loaf sugar
1½ oz bruised root ginger
1 oz cream of tartar
2 lemons, rind and juice
3 gallons boiling water
2 large tablesp fresh yeast
a piece of toast

Put rind and juice of lemons, bruised ginger, sugar and cream of tartar into an earthen pan and pour boiling water over them. Let it stand until just warm, then add yeast and stir well. Put in a piece of toast, this will gather the yeast. Let the mixture stand by the fire all night, covering the pan with a cloth. Next morning skim off the yeast and bottle the liquid, leaving all sediment at the bottom of the pan. Tie down the corks and in three days the beer will be fit for use.

Seed cake features prominently in all the old recipe books I have looked through, some containing several versions. It must have been an adult taste, so many of us remember detesting it as children! Elma Banks includes it in her selection as a typical haytiming cake -

SEED CAKE   (Aunt Janie's maid Lily's recipe)

8 oz flour   1 teasp baking powder
4 oz butter   6 oz sugar
2 eggs   about 1 teacupful milk
1 dessertsp caraway seeds

Bake about 1 hour in 'not too quick an oven'

Bannocks (or Nodden cakes) were carried by the men who worked in the mines and quarries, as the main part of their bait. Also popular with children, and at haytime. Another type was made into rounds about 8" diameter, split, buttered and spread with jam while hot.

GAYLE BANNOCKS   (Mary Bell)

8 oz flour   4 oz lard
salt   water

Rub lard into flour and make into a dough with the water. Roll out about quarter inch thick then cut into 2" squares. Place on a baking tray and bake in moderate hot oven.
Served cold, buttered and with treacle (often for breakfast)

FAT RASCALS (Mrs Clapham)

1 lb flour
half cup currants
1 heaped teasp baking powder

8 oz lard
1 dessertsp sugar

Rub lard into flour. Add rest, mix to a dough with a little milk. Roll out and cut into rounds. Bake brown on both sides in a hot oven. Split, butter and serve hot.

EASTER CAKES (Mary Bell)

3 oz butter
6 oz flour
1 egg

3 oz caster sugar
2 oz clean dry currants
pinch cinnamon

Beat butter to a cream, then mix in sugar, flour, cinnamon and currants. Make into a paste with beaten egg. Roll out thinly and cut into rounds. Sprinkle with caster sugar, bake on greased baking trays in moderate oven until slightly browned.

CHOC-CRUNCH COOKIES (Isobel Leyland)

4 oz butter or marge melted with a **6 oz slab of stoneless dates.** Pursue round pan with a wooden spoon. *(That's what it says!)* Stir in **3 oz rice crispies,** press mixture into a 6" by 10" tin to half inch thickness. Cover with **4 oz melted cooking chocolate.** It cuts when cool into 18 goodly portions.

LEMON CURD TARTS (Beatrice Irving)

These tarts, along with cheesecakes, were her mother Mrs Guy Routh's speciality at Chapel bazaars and tea parties.

2 oz butter
1 egg
shortcrust pastry

6 oz caster sugar
juice of 1 lemon

Cream butter and sugar until fluffy, add beaten egg, then lemon juice. Line 4 saucers with shortcrust pastry then add the mixture. Bake at 350°F for 20 mins.

URPETH GINGER SNAPS   (Peg Scarr)

1 lb flour   ½ lb butter or marge
1 lb treacle   ¼ lb sugar
pinch salt   pinch bicarb. soda
2 teasp ground ginger

Mix dry ingredients together. Boil butter and treacle, then pour over.
Mix well, set aside until cold, then roll out thinly and bake.

GRANNY PRESTON'S GINGER BISCUITS
Made at West End House for over 100 years.

2 breakfast cups plain flour   1 breakfast cup sugar
3 oz butter   1 oz lard
1 tablesp syrup   3 teasp ground ginger
¼ teasp salt
1 teasp carb. soda scalded in 1½ tablesp boiling water

Rub the fats into the flour and salt, add sugar, mix with syrup and
scalded carb. soda to a stiff paste.   Roll out thinly, cut into rounds
(Granny used a glass tumbler) and bake until golden.

OAT BISCUITS *(Granny Preston's, from an Askrigg recipe book
produced before 1914) This is still a popular recipe.   If you do not
bake bread and so do not have spare dough to use, these biscuits can
be bought at Cockett's in Hawes .*

8 oz bread dough   8 oz Quaker oats
2 oz butter   2 oz lard
pinch of salt   small teasp baking powder

Bake until crisp but not brown. Serve buttered.

Frieze on panelling at West End House, said to have been brought from Lady Anne Clifford's Pendragon Castle in
Mallerstang when it was dismantled in the 18th century.

AUNTIE GLADYS BISCUITS

5 oz butter or margarine   5 oz granulated sugar
5 oz plain flour   4 oz rolled oats
1 teasp baking powder   ½ teasp bicarb. soda
1 dessertsp syrup   2 tablesp milk

Cream butter and sugar, add syrup, then flour, baking powder and soda, next milk and lastly oats. Put small spoonfuls on baking sheets, allowing room to spread. Bake at 360ºF for about 10 mins until brown. Allow to cool on tin for a few minutes before removing to cooling tray. Store in a plastic bag in a tin.

S.O.S. CAKE   (Mrs T.E. Metcalfe senior)

1½ cups flour   ½ cup ground rice
1 cup sugar   5 oz marge
2 eggs   8 oz currants
half cup milk   2 teasp baking powder

YORKSHIRE PARKINS   (Margaret Hopper)

7 oz flour   4 oz oatmeal
3 oz butter or lard   2 oz demerara sugar
2 oz mixed spice   pinch of nutmeg
6 oz treacle   1 teasp milk
½ teasp bicarb. soda

Rub butter into flour, add sugar, oatmeal and spice. Pour in hot syrup, add carb. soda dissolved in the milk. Form into balls the size of an egg, place in greased tin allowing room to spread slightly. Brush over with milk and bake about 15 min in a slow oven.

GINGERBREAD   (Margaret Ann *(Granny)* Preston)

1 lb flour   1 teasp baking powder
½ lb sugar, sifted   2 eggs
½ lb treacle   1 or 2 teasp ground ginger
½ lb butter or lard   milk *if not moist enough*

(No method!)

STICKY PARKIN

(Muriel Towler)

6 oz self-raising flour	6 oz medium oatmeal
3 oz sugar	½ pt milk
8 oz syrup	3 oz lard or margarine
1 flat teasp bicarb. soda	
1 heaped teasp ground ginger	

Melt margarine and syrup, warm the milk (reserving a little to mix with the bicarb) and mix all the ingredients together. Pour into a greased roasting tin and bake at 325°F to 350°F for 1 to 1¼ hours. *This improves after a few days when it will become deliciously sticky. No bonfire night is complete without parkin and...*

TREACLE TOFFEE

(Margaret Hopper)

1 lb black treacle - or half treacle, half golden syrup	
¼ lb butter	2 tablesp water
1 lb sugar	1 tablesp vinegar

Put all ingredients in a heavy pan. Heat gently until sugar is melted then boil about 20 mins until, when a portion is dropped into cold water, it crackles. Pour onto a tin lined with baking parchment and leave until cool, then press lines with a knife to make portions.

CHEESE-CAKE, that is curd cheese rather than the biscuit-crumb-and-cream-cheese of recent years, is a local speciality, although they make a similar curd tart in the West Riding.. Cheese cakes are included in most mediaeval cookbooks, using such ingredients as rosewater, nutmeg and breadcrumbs. Some used egg yolks and no whites, another delicious-sounding recipe used egg-whites mixed with elderflowers.

Mary Dinsdale, who with her husband Tom (well known as the walking-stick maker) farmed at Dale Foot, Bishopdale until their retirement, is known throughout the dale for her cheesecakes.

CHEESECAKE   (Mary Dinsdale)

shortcrust pastry	2 eggs
½ lb curd	½ lb sugar
¼ lb butter	3 oz currants
1 dessertsp cream	a little rum

Cream butter and sugar - add eggs, curd and currants.   Finally add cream.   Put in tins lined with shortcrust pastry and bake in a moderate oven.   Leave to cool, then pour on a little rum.

There seem to be as many cheesecake recipes as there are cheesecake makers, so here with her slight variations, and directions on how to make the curds is "Auntie Calvert's" from Elizabeth Metcalfe in Askrigg

YORKSHIRE CHEESECAKES

Curd; Take **one pint of warm milk** and add **half a teaspoonful of rennet.**   Let this stand for an hour, then cut the curd and drain in muslin until all the whey is out.

Cheese cake filling: To each **6 oz of curd** add **3 oz of sugar,   2 oz of currants, 4 oz of butter or margarine, nutmeg, a pinch of salt and one egg.**

Method: Beat the curd until fine, then add sugar, fruit, nutmeg, egg and salt and finally the butter or margarine which has been softened to a cream.   Have ready tins lined with soft pastry and fill these with the mixture.   Flavour with rum if desired.

Mary Johnson's SPONGE CAKE *from Marian Kirby, who remembers Auntie Mary beating it for 20 minutes. She was the daughter of the miller at Yore Mill, Aysgarth and made teas for the tourists who came to visit Aysgarth Falls by train excursion, charabanc, car and bicycle in the 1920s and 30s.*

Three quarters of a pound of loaf sugar melted on the fire in a teacupful of water
7 eggs (leaving out three whites)
Beat the eggs a little then pour the boiling water on them and beat (20 mins!)
Then add **half a pound of flour and a little baking powder.**
Stir the flour very lightly - if you beat the flour in you will spoil your cake. Bake in a quick oven for one hour.

These cakes were baked in tin jelly moulds, well greased, floured and sugared, and turned out with almost every bump perfect!

A fascinating forerunner to this book is the LEYBURN COOKERY BOOK which belonged to Mary's mother Ethel Johnson in 1907. With tiny pages of deckle-edge paper it was produced to raise money for a new piano for the church. The contributions range from Sheep's Head and Brain sauce, and "Nurse Rhodes' Easily Digested Steamed Chop", to such sophisticated fare as Creamed Lobster. It was a surprise to me to find that Maggi stock cubes and tinned prawns used in one recipe, were available then. The following dish from A. Brigham sounds tasty - whether served on its own as a vegetarian dish, or as an accompaniment to pork.

VEGETABLE GOOSE

Take a good-sized **vegetable marrow** and boil until tender. Plunge into cold water and peel. Take off one end in the shape of a stopper, remove seeds etc, stuff with **sage and onions** and replace stopper. Place on a greased tin, dredge with flour and bake until nicely browned, basting well.
Serve with **gravy and apple sauce.**

I could not resist including this, which makes one appreciate what a performance it must have been to preserve meat without refrigeration. It sounds somewhat unscientific, I can't imagine that it really worked!

TO PICKLE MEAT IN ONE DAY   (Lizzie Scott)

Fill a tub or bowl full of rain or river water, put two pieces of stick across the top, and lay the beef upon them at a distance of about an inch from the water.   Heap as much salt as possible on the beef and leave it for 24 hours.   Take the meat off and boil it, and it will be just as salt as if it had been in pickle for six weeks.   The water draws the salt through.

And this one which conjures up visions of Chapel teas, or perhaps of the great Tea Festivals which were held on Leyburn Shawl in the 19th century

TEMPERANCE CAKE   (E.Spence)

1¼ lbs flour, ¾ lb currants, ¾ lb sugar, ½ lb butter or lard, 2 oz candied peel, one small nutmeg, one dessertsp carbonate of soda mixed in ½ pint of butter-milk, lastly two dessertsp of vinegar.

SPONGE CAKE   (Another version from Marian Kirby out of a different family book)

Take **6 very fresh eggs.**   The weight of **five** of them in **sugar,** of **three** in very fine dry **flour.**   Put the sugar into a shallow flat dish, and break the eggs onto it.   Be careful to remove the stringy part of the yolk, this always makes a cake heavy.   Add to this the **grated rind of a small lemon,** and beat the whole for 20 minutes.   Then sift in the flour stirring as lightly as possible til all is mixed in.   Put in a well-buttered dish and oven immediately.

LEMON CREAM   (from the same book but in a different hand)
Take **a pint of thick cream** and put to it **the yolks of three eggs well beaten 4 oz of fine sugar and the thin rind of a lemon** well grated boil stir it till almost cold put the juice of a lemon in a dish and pour the cream upon it stirring it till quite cold it is excellent when iced.   *(From mediæval times punctuation has been of little importance to the cook!)*

76

WIN'S GROUND RICE TARTS

Line patty tins with rounds of **short pastry** and small spoonfuls of **raspberry jam.** Cream **2 oz butter with 2 oz caster sugar**, add **1 beaten egg and 2 oz ground rice.** Put a teaspoon of the mixture over the tarts,and bake in a moderate oven until brown.

JOAN'S CHEESE SCONES

1½ cups grated Wensleydale cheese
1 small cup plain flour   2 teasp baking powder
½ teasp salt   1 egg and a little milk

Bake no longer than 5 mins, top shelf, Gas 6-7

CHOCOLATE WALNUT BISCUITS   W.H.R.

3 oz margarine   2 oz sugar
4 oz self-raising flour   1 oz cornflakes
3 teasp cocoa powder   vanilla essence

Beat fat and sugar, add dry ingredients. Roll out and cut with small cutter. Bake 20 mins in medium oven. Ice with a blob of cocoa-flavoured icing and top with a piece of walnut. *(When iced they are soon inclined to soften , so if keeping suggest melted chocolate.)*

AFTERNOON TEA SCONES
(Mrs Kettlewell,
Rose & Crown, Bainbridge
around 1925)

1 lb flour
4 oz butter
4 tablesp caster sugar
2 teasp cream of tartar
1 teasp carb. soda
4 eggs
a little cold water

Rub the butter lightly into the flour and add the remaining dry ingredients. Beat then stir in the eggs, adding cold water or milk to make a light dough. Roll out thin and cut into small rounds. Bake in a hot oven.

"Daddy was trying not to take a piece of mint and currant pasty to eat with his cup of tea, but he was reading the paper at the same time and his hand was going to take the wrong thing if it could. Mother twisted the plate so that he would take a mince pie instead. When Jimmy came in and said 'She's sat on one', Daddy looked up and took the pasty, bit it and said he didn't like it."

Many of William Mayne's incomparable books for children have a Dales setting. This is from The Changeling (1961). Daddy is in the minority, most people enjoy the fresh flavour.

MINT AND CURRANT PASTY

shortcrust pastry	lemon juice
2 oz butter	2 oz sugar
2-3 tablesp chopped mint	3 oz currants

Cream butter and sugar, add currants, mint and a squeeze of lemon juice. Roll out pastry to a rectangle, spread mixture over half, double over the other half and crimp the damped edges together. Bake until crisp. Slice when cold.

Countersett .   Janet Rawlins

TEA LOAF, TO BUTTER (Margaret Hopper)

7½ oz self-raising flour
1½ oz sugar
1½ tablesp syrup
3 oz dates
pinch salt
½ teasp bicarb. soda
nutmeg to flavour
1½ cups milk added cold

Bake slowly for about 1½ hours

Unfortunately many of the writers of recipes assumed they were writing for experienced cooks and that instructions as to method were superfluous. Ella Tennant's grandmother gives the ingredients for a 'teaday loaf" using a STONE of flour, but at a later day has written in the quantities for a mere four loaves.....

TEADAY LOAF (Mrs J. Hodgson)

4 lbs flour
1 lb sugar
1 pt new milk
½ lb butter or butter and lard mixed
A penny-ha'penny of yeast - *and,*
 - wait for it -
"as many eggs as you think"!

1½ lbs currants
¼ lb lemon peel

BANANA TEA BREAD (Ella Metcalfe)

8 oz self-raising flour
4 oz margarine or butter
1 oz walnuts
1 lb bananas, fairly ripe
8 oz dried fruit (dates, raisins etc)

½ teasp salt
6 oz white sugar
2 eggs

Rub fat into flour, add sugar and dried fruit.   Mix in beaten eggs. Mash bananas, add to mixture and pour into two small or one large baking tin, putting the walnuts on top. Bake at 300F for 1½ hours. Cool before removing from tins. Keep for a few days before using. Serve buttered if liked.

79

KITCHEN CAKE   (Mrs J. Hodgson)

1 lb flour	8 oz sugar
4 oz raisins	4 oz currants
8 oz butter or lard	1 cup milk
1 teasp bicarb. soda	

Put soda into flour dry. Melt fat.

SPONGE SANDWICH   (Peggy Storey)

3 eggs, the weight of 1 in butter, 2 in flour, 3 in sugar. Beat the eggs.
Sugar.
*This was jotted down, in the 19th century, in the margin of an 18th
century farm record book written in a beautiful copper-plate hand.
Probably the only handy bit of paper!*

SPICE BREAD   (Mary Braithwaite)

1 lb flour	1 oz yeast
4 oz butter	4 oz lard
1 lb brown sugar	8 oz currants
8 oz raisins	1 teasp carb. soda
2 eggs	a little milk
a pinch of spice, or nutmeg	

Rub fat into flour, add rest of dry ingredients. Warm milk and let
yeast rise in it, then add beaten eggs to yeast/milk. Mix all together,
finally add carbonate of soda in a little tepid milk. Half fill 2 cake
tins and bake in slow oven 2 - 2½ hours. (350ºF, reducing to 325ºF)
Serve buttered.

DATE AND WALNUT CAKE

1 large tablesp butter	1 breakfast cup sugar
1 cup sour milk	1 egg
1 teasp carb soda	pinch of salt
1 cup chopped dates	2 cups self-raising flour
½ cup chopped walnuts	

Cream together butter and sugar. Add dry ingredients and carb
soda mixed with a little milk. Bake in a slow oven (gas 4) reducing
to (gas 3)

SPONGE FUNERAL BISCUITS   (Ella Tennant, Worton Hall)

½ lb flour
3 eggs
½ teasp baking powder

½ lb sugar
pinch salt
drop of vanilla

Drop good teaspoonfuls on to greased baking sheet and bake in a slow oven.

In Swaledale two of these biscuits were wrapped in a new black-bordered handkerchief and given to each of the bearers before the funeral.

YORKSHIRE TEACAKES

2½ lb flour
3 oz sugar
2 level teasp salt
1 pt milk

4 oz fat
2 oz yeast
a few currants

Rub fat into flour and salt. Add sugar. Make milk nice and hot but not boiling. Put a little over the flour and the rest over the yeast. Work lightly. Rise about 1 hour to twice its size. Then place in shapes on oven shelf. Rise about half to one hour. Bake 10 to 15 min only in a hot oven.

81

YULE CAKE and YULE CAKES (See Section I, 19th century). *The first Margaret Hopper's, the second from Alice Chapman's recipe book from the 1920s. Entirely different as one uses yeast and the other eggs, both somewhat short on detail!*

YULE CAKE   (Margaret Hopper)

3½ lb flour   1 lb fat
1 lb sugar   1 lb stoned raisins
1 lb currants   ¼ lb mixed peel
a little salt   teasp carb. soda
4 oz yeast

Mix with warm milk, add a little cinnamon or nutmeg.

YULE CAKES   (Alice Chapman)

2 lbs flour   ¾ lb lard
¼ lb butter   3 eggs
1 lb sugar   a little cream
season with nutmeg

(another recipe adds a fourth egg and 1 lb currants)

Mrs Ballardie's CHRISTMAS CAKE

10 oz flour   2 oz glacé cherries
2 oz almonds   ¼ nutmeg
a little milk   8 oz raisins
8 oz currants   8 oz sugar
8 oz butter   3 eggs
1 teasp baking powder

Beat butter and sugar, add eggs, then fruit and grated nutmeg, and sieve in flour. Mix well.   Line the tin, and bake in a moderate oven about 2 hours.   (Test with a skewer; when it comes out clean the cake is done.)

Served, traditionally, with chunks of **Wensleydale cheese.**

𝕮𝖆𝖓𝖉𝖎𝖉 𝖕𝖊𝖊𝖑   (Emma Clifford Bilton)

(Billie's spelling!)

The elderly Miss Bilton (Billie) lived in a 17th century manor house in Wharfedale in the 1930s and 40s and claimed to be a descendant of Lady Anne Clifford's family. This rather time-consuming recipe is written in purple ink with numerous flourishes.

½ lb orange peel - about 5 oranges,
1 lb sugar
¼ pt water

Cover the peel (cut in quarters) with cold water & a tiny pinch of salt. Leave overnight. <u>Drain</u>. Cover again with cold water & bring slowly to the boil, let simmer very slowly all day or as long as possible, drain thoroughly. Cover again with cold water & pinch of salt. <u>Drain</u> thoroughly. Repeat this process until the peel is quite soft but not broken.
Boil 1 lb caster sugar with the water <u>not</u> until candied only melted. Add well drained peel & simmer very slowly until peel has absorbed practically all the syrup. Stir it gently occasionally it does not burn easily. Toss onto a well-sugared paper - toss occasionally until cold.

83

LEMON CHEESE
(Auntie Calvert's, from Elizabeth Metcalfe)

1 lb loaf sugar broken into small pieces
¼ lb butter.
6 eggs, leaving out two whites
the grated rind of 3 lemons and juice of same

Put all into a pan and simmer over fire until it is
dissolved and begins to thicken like honey.

HORSE RADISH SAUCE (Margaret Hopper)

1½ oz horseradish
1 small tin evaporated milk and
                  1 dessertsp sugar, <u>or</u>
1 small tin sweet condensed milk
1 tablesp white vinegar
½ teasp salt
½ teasp mixed mustard

Grate or mince the prepared
horseradish, stir in the milk,
add salt and mustard then
vinegar (if liked more vinegar
may be added). Put in jars
with good screw tops and this
will keep it well. If sterilised
it will keep indefinitely.

PARSLEY HONEY
(Margaret Hopper)

May be used as a preserve with bread and butter, but is also an
excellent accompaniment with cold meat, especially chicken.. Fill a
preserving pan with **fresh parsley leaves.** Scarcely cover with
cold water, bring to the boil and simmer gently for 1 hour. Add
**juice of 1 lemon plus the thinly peeled rind to every pint of
liquid.** Cool, then strain. Measure, **and to each pint of juice
add 1 lb of sugar.** Return to the pan and boil until jelly sets when
tested on a cold plate. Pour into jars and cover when quite cold.

MINT SAUCE FOR WINTER KEEPING   (Margaret Hopper)

1 pt vinegar   1 lb sugar   ½ lb mint leaves

Weigh the mint leaves which have been gathered fresh, clean and dry. Put them through the mincer . Boil the vinegar, add sugar and reboil. Pour this over the minced leaves in a basin, stirring well with a wooden spoon.   Leave to go cold, stirring frequently.   Put into screw top jars. Will keep for months.   To use, remove as much mint as required and add more vinegar.

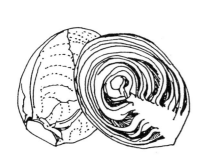 

PICKLED RED CABBAGE   (Alice Chapman)
Slightly frost-bitten cabbages make the best pickle

Quarter and remove the core, and cut the cabbage across into extremely fine shreds. Leave it spread on a dish with plenty of salt between the layers for 24 hours, then drain with pressure.   To each quart of vinegar add a teaspoonful of peppercorns and allspice, a small root of ginger and a quarter teasp cayenne.   Boil vinegar and spices together for 15 mins and when quite cold pour over the cabbage in jars, distributing the spices.   It will be ready for use in a week.

GRANNY OUTHWAITE'S SPICED PEPPER
from Carr End, Raydaleside

½ lb white pepper	**½ oz ground mace**
¼ oz cayenne pepper	**1 oz ground nutmeg**
1 oz ground cloves	**2 oz black pepper**

As spices soon lose their potency after grinding, I wonder how quickly this quantity was used up!

WENSLEYDALE CHEESE

Cheese and butter were made by the farmer's wife on most dales farms, then in 1897 Edward Chapman of Hawes started to buy milk from the farms and to make cheese on a larger scale.

By the 1930s the dairy was facing closure when Kit Calvert came to the rescue by forming a company of local people with himself as managing director. In 1966 the business was bought by Dairy Crest, and most people know of their shock decision in 1992 to close the creamery with a loss of 59 jobs, and to make Wensleydale cheese in Lancashire! Once again there was a rescue bid, and now in 1993 cheese is again being made in Upper Wensleydale and winning national prizes. The Hawes factory now uses milk from herds fed on local pastures, and in addition to the regular Wensleydale makes Mature, Blue and Smoked Wensleydale (as well as other cheeses).

COVERDALE CHEESE, a slightly firmer texture, is made along with WENSLEYDALE at the Kirby Malzeard dairy, not far from Jervaulx Abbey.

A farmhouse style SWALEDALE CHEESE is made at a small factory in Richmond from both cows milk and the original ewes milk.

A farmhouse WENSLEYDALE is made in Thirsk from ewes milk, where they also make a WHARFEDALE cheese.

GOATS CHEESE is made at Ribblehead.

All these can be obtained at Elijah Allen in Hawes, where Basil and Richard Allen will advise, and at specialist cheese shops in many areas.

86

The Scarr family have owned Coleby Hall since the 1930s, but have farmed there for 300 years. Cheeses were made by Mrs Mary Scarr during and after the First World War and posted all over the country to the friends and relatives of Mr Harold Lowther the then owner.

WENSLEYDALE CHEESE   (Eleanor Scarr, Coleby Hall)

**4 gallons milk   1 drachm (⅛ oz) rennet
salt - 1 oz to 3 lbs curd.**   Warm the milk to 86°F, add rennet. Stir deeply for 5 mins and afterwards on the surface, stopping when there are signs of coagulation. After approx 1 hour the curd should split clean, leaving no particles on your fingers. Cut lengthways and crossways with a knife. If the curd is too soft scalding will help, by adding boiling water until the temperature is up to between 86°F and 90°F.   Strain off the whey and cut the curd in small pieces. Weigh, and add salt, 1 oz to 3 lbs curd, working well in with hands. The cheese is now ready to put in a mould and stand overnight before pressing for one day. Wrap cheese cloth round the cheese and put back into the mould for a short time to press on the cloth. Dry on a wooden shelf, turning daily. Ready to eat in 3 to 4 weeks. (At this age a gallon of milk can yield up to 1¼ lbs of cheese, but more usually 17 or 18 oz. If kept for 4 to 5 months to go blue, the yield is usually about 14 oz cheese from a gallon.)

Many farms had a cheese room, often over the dairy which was cool. The one at West End House (now a bedroom but still called the Cheese Room) had no windows, but had a doorway accessible by ladder from the yard so that after drying out on slatted shelves the cheeses could be loaded directly on to a cart..

*This excerpt from Jane Gardam's 1981 Whitbread award-winning novel **The Hollow Land** is typical of the life of many daleswomen in the early part of this century. 'Granny Crack' has decided she has had enough and retired - to bed.....*

"Worked all her life - up before five every morning, milking fifty years, never a holiday in all her life. Right away up on Kisdon we lived, miles from nowhere. Made her own butter and cheese and bread. Fed the nine of us out of twenty five shilling a week - my father was a pig killer till he died, going round the farms killing and helping here and there hay-times, as we did, us and mother too, carrying pots of stew on harnesses on our backs away up the fell. Such a cook she was! She'd fill a big black pot - one of them with bright, thick silver insides - with potatoes and onions and carrots and a bone, and cover it with water and boil it up slow. Beautiful. Every day oft' week, and bread and syrup for supper. Sundays there'd may be a spare rib pie. Proper spare rib, not this so called spare rib now. And a crust over it. She could heft the sheep and clip the sheep and dip. She could salt the pig and make sausage and black puddings. She could stack a rick of hay and corn and she could paint a house inside and out and mend the great roof tiles. She could milk and separate and calve a cow. She never had a day's sickness in her life, no more had we. We never saw a doctor. She had us out of our beds six o'clock each day including Sunday, and she was always last to bed at night. And look at her now."

From Marie Hartley and Joan Ingilby's
'LIFE AND TRADITION IN THE YORKSHIRE DALES' (1988)

"In this century, farmhouse kitchens are still comfortable places; but perhaps the 'house' was at its best fifty years ago when large families were brought up, when little was bought, when hams and sides of bacon, pickled beef, herbs and charms such as strings of blown eggs or witchstones were hung up to ward off evil spirits, when home-made butter and cheese, bread and cheese cakes filled the dairy, and havercake found a place on ceiling-boards together with caps, hats and boots.   But what work it represented!"

SECTION III
FOOD FROM THE DALES COUNTRYSIDE

This dales countryside has trout streams, grouse moors, sheep and cattle farming. Edible wild plants may be less common here in a landscape of stone walls than in parts of the country where hedgerows survive. None the less there is luxuriant growth in places protected from the voracious appetites of sheep. Most of the following plants and flowers can be found along pathways and quiet roadsides. Avoid collecting them where there may be danger of pollution from passing traffic. Do not gather any but the most common flowers - I have mentioned some such as primroses and violets which are far less common now, so please, grow some in the garden to preserve and leave the wild ones for others to enjoy. These edible plants are listed more or less in seasonal order.

I have not included recipes for home-made wines as this seems to be a subject which would require a book all to itself.

Several of these recipes come from WILD FOOD by Roger Phillips who knows Wensleydale well. I am grateful for his permission to use them.

91

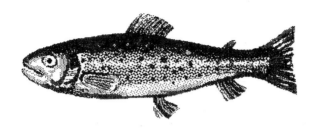

TROUT   Dales rivers are famed for their brown trout, but for those who do not fish there are trout farms at Gayle in Wensleydale and Kilnsey in Wharfedale (where one can also buy smoked trout and frozen game birds).

TROUT AND PRAWN PARCELS
from **Gill Moore** of Blackburn Farm trout fishery at Gayle.

4 medium trout, preferably boned
half a cucumber, de-seeded and cut into strips
12 prawns   lemon juice   salt & black pepper

Place cucumber in a colander and sprinkle with salt. Leave 15 mins, rinse, drop in boiling water for 2 mins. Drain and refresh under cold running water. Leave to drain.   Mix cucumber with prawns and 1 tablesp chopped parsley and stuff the trout.
Place each trout on a piece of buttered foil. Season well and sprinkle with lemon juice. Wrap up each parcel loosely but well sealed and place on baking tray. Cook 20 mins at 375ºF/190ºC. Serve the parcels on heated plates with freshly baked bread to soak up the juices.

GRAYLING

These fish are said to smell of thyme when newly caught. Cook in the same way as trout; grill, poach or bake.

93

CRAYFISH.

Old guide books claim that these were introduced into the river Ure by Sir Walter Raleigh when on a visit to Nappa Hall. A highly unlikely but romantic notion! They seem less abundant than a few years ago, possibly pollution is responsible. The traditional way to catch them is to tie a piece of meat or kipper to a string and dangle this in the beck or river. The crayfish will cling to the kipper...and to your finger if it gets the chance. Like lobsters they are dropped into boiling water to cook, and are done when they turn red, in about seven minutes

RABBITS and HARES (recipes in other sections) can usually be obtained from local butchers.

As can **GROUSE, PARTRIDGE, and PHEASANT**
if you do not happen to have part-share in a grouse moor! (recipes in other sections)

JACK-BY-THE-HEDGE or Garlic Mustard

One of the earliest and most common plants to appear along our roadsides and as a weed in the garden. Garlicky flavour; use the young small leaves sparingly in salads, cook as a vegetable. Add a few chopped leaves or the dried seeds to casseroles.

CHICKWEED
Chickweed has a pleasant peppery taste and can be eaten in salads, or boiled as a vegetable. *(Will weeding ever be the same again?)*

FAT HEN and it's relative
GOOD-KING-HENRY
Use the leaves in salads or cook like spinach. The young shoots can be boiled and eaten like asparagus. It has been used as a vegetable since Neolithic times.

DANDELIONS
Use young leaves in salads. Try blanching some in the garden under an old bucket If you are really keen you can dig up the roots in autumn and dry them to make dandelion coffee.

NETTLES
Pick the young nettle tops (just the top 5 to 6 cm, 2"- 3") for
NETTLE SOUP

450 g (1 lb) potatoes	**225 g (8 oz) nettle tops**
50 g (2 oz) butter	
900 ml (1½ pts) chicken stock	
salt and black pepper	**small carton sour cream**

Peel and slice potatoes. Wash thoroughly and coarsely chop nettles. Cook potatoes in salted water for 10 mins, drain. Melt butter in saucepan, add nettles and stew gently for 10 mins, add potatoes and heated stock, bring to boil and simmer a further 10 mins. Purée in a blender, return to a clean pan, reheat and add sour cream.
(Alternatively add a sliced leek, and use half a pint of milk in place of the soured cream)

NETTLE PURÉE WITH EGGS

4 large eggs	**675 g (1½ lbs) young nettle tops**
40 g (1½ oz) butter	**4 tablesp double cream**
sea salt and black pepper	

Bring a pan of lightly salted water to the boil and add eggs. Cook 5 minutes, hold under cold tap and shell. Keep in bowl of hot water.

95

Cook nettle tops in large pan of lightly salted boiling water , or steam them. Drain thoroughly, chop finely preferably in a food processor. Reheat in a clean pan, adding butter, cream and seasoning. Spoon into 4 ramekins and top with the (dried) soft-boiled eggs.

RAMSONS (wild garlic)

Use young spring leaves chopped in salads, the starry flowers and the young green berries as garnish.

ROCAMBOLE

Look for it along roadsides. It has a strong garlic flavour and an attractive seed head. Not common enough to pick these days, but try collecting a few seeds to grow in the garden.

WOODRUFF

Add a sprig of partially dried woodruff to apple juice for a delicious summer drink.
Fresh or dried woodruff makes a stimulating tea,
or in the spring make
Maywine - Pick a small bunch of woodruff. Rinse, shake dry, and hang in a warm place for a few hours. Then put in a bowl with a dessert spoonful of caster sugar, the juice of a lemon and its pared rind, and a bottle of dry white wine. Leave in a warm place for three hours, then strain and chill. When serving add carbonated spring water - or sparkling wine.

WOOD SORREL
A few of the pretty shamrock-shaped
leaves add piquancy to a salad.

SORREL   Commonly found on grassland.
Add to salads.   It goes well with trout. (See page 41 for Sorrel and
Gooseberry Sauce.) *Don't eat a lot if you suffer from rheumatism..*

SORREL SOUP.   serves 4   (Roger Phillips)

large handful washed sorrel leaves
1 small lettuce, or chickweed
1 large onion, chopped   **12 g (½ oz butter)**
1 large potato   **3 dl (½ pt milk)**
1 ltr (1½ pts) chicken stock
salt and pepper

Melt the butter in a large saucepan, add the leaves and onion and
soften without browning. Add the potato and boiling stock (or cube +
water). Simmer uncovered for 20 to 30 minutes until the potato is
cooked. Sieve or liquidise for a few seconds. Add milk and
seasoning. Heat through and serve with fried croutons.

HAWTHORN   (May blossom) can be crystallised
(see section IV)

HAWTHORN BRANDY (1822)
(Margaret Hopper)

Take a large bottle, fill with
hawthorn petals, (flowers only,
no stalks) picked when the day
is dry and sunny. Fill up with
brandy.   Let it infuse for 5 to
6 weeks, then strain off the
liquid.   This imparts a
delicious flavour to puddings,
sweets etc.

SWEET CICELY

This herb grows abundantly along roadsides in Wensleydale, it looks like a luxuriant cow parsley and when crushed the leaves smell strongly of aniseed. Use in salads and as a garnish (salmon looks wonderful on a bed of the frondy leaves) and in summer drinks. Crystallise the leaves as decoration for cakes and puddings. Chop green seed heads and add to whipped cream. Leaves, flowers and seed heads are all attractive with cut flowers (to prevent the leaves from going limp immerse them in cold water for an hour or so).

In the 16th and 17th century the roots were eaten boiled like parsnips. Some books mention the crushed seeds being used to polish furniture but I have not had much success with this.

Deep fry in batter (see Comfrey) for an exotic appetiser.

Add a few chopped leaves when cooking rhubarb, apples or gooseberries and far less sugar will be needed. (Or a handful of whole leaves, which you can squeeze and remove after cooking.)

COMFREY grows in damp places and on roadsides. It has been used in wound-healing since the Middle Ages. The young leaves can be cooked and eaten like spinach. (There is recent concern about eating large quantities so although I have given a number of recipes don't try them all at once!)

COMFREY QUICHE Serves 4 - 6

100 g (¼ lb) shortcrust pastry
2 eggs   salt
1.5 dl (¼ pt) single cream
freshly milled pepper
450 g (1 lb) comfrey leaves
50 g (2 oz) grated Wensleydale cheese

Wash the comfrey leaves well and steam, or simmer in a very little water until tender. Squeeze out any remaining juice and mash or blend. Roll out the pastry and line an 8 in. flan ring.
Fill with crumpled foil and bake 'blind' for 10 - 15 minutes.
Whisk together the eggs and cream, season. Mix in the comfrey and fill the pastry case. Sprinkle on the grated cheese .
Bake in centre of moderate hot oven 375ºF 190ºC gas 5 for 40 - 45 mins until set firm. Serve warm.

COMFREY AND PEANUT   serves 4
                              (Roger Phillips)

50 g (2 oz) sunflower oil
100 g (4 oz) onion, peeled and chopped
50 g (2 oz) unsalted peanuts
450 g (1 lb) comfrey leaves

Heat the oil in a pan, add the onion and sauté until lightly brown. Add the peanuts and cook for 2 minutes, then add the comfrey leaves and sauté for about 15 minutes until all the liquid has been absorbed. Season well with salt and pepper.

COMFREY FRITTERS   serves 4   (Roger Phillips)

100 g (4 oz) flour
½ dl (¼ pt) tepid water
comfrey leaves
1 egg
pinch salt, cayenne pepper
hot fat for frying

Separate the egg-white from the yolk. Sieve the flour and salt into a basin, make a well in the centre and drop in the yolk. Add the water, mixing it in gradually with a wooden spoon, work in the flour and leave to stand. Lastly, whip the egg-white to a froth and fold it in. Pick the comfrey leaves with a small amount of stalk, wash and dry well and dip the leaves into the batter. Deep fry in hot fat until golden brown on both sides. Drain on paper towels and serve sprinkled with salt and cayenne pepper.

GROUND ELDER
Said to have been introduced by the Romans, and grown as a vegetable in the Middle Ages. If you are pestered by it as a weed you can at least eat it. Cook like spinach.

WATERCRESS

In this sheep farming country there is a danger of catching liver fluke from wild watercress. However it is quite safe to eat after cooking.

WATERCRESS SOUP   (Roger Phillips)

2 bunches watercress
2 large potatoes, sliced
a generous knob butter
a dash of vegetable oil (to stop butter burning)
1 chicken stock cube, dissolved in
1 pt boiling water
salt and freshly ground black pepper
single cream

Put butter in a large saucepan with a dash of oil and melt over low heat. Cook very gently until potatoes are softening but not brown. Add stock and simmer 15 mins, then add coarsely chopped watercress (keeping a few choice leaves for garnish) and simmer a further 7 mins. Liquidise. Serve hot or cold with dash of cream.

ELDER

Elder trees were always planted outside houses, privies and dairies to keep away, conveniently, both flies and witches! They are common everywhere and their flowers and fruit among the most useful of our wild harvest, so I make no apology for getting somewhat carried away with elder recipes.

ELDERFLOWER FRITTERS

Shake but do not wash flower heads. See COMFREY for recipe

ELDERFLOWER WITH GOOSEBERRIES

Tie a few elderflower heads in a piece of muslin and stew with gooseberries and sugar to taste - it has a delightful muscat flavour.

ELDERFLOWER PANCAKES

100 g (4 oz) plain flour
pinch of salt
1 teasp caster sugar
½ teasp grated orange peel
2 eggs
300 ml (½ pt) milk
4 stripped heads of elderflowers
2 tablesp melted butter
juice of 1 orange or lemon
runny honey

Blend all ingredients except the last four until smooth. Add elderflowers and leave to stand at least half an hour. Stir in melted butter. Pour a tablespoonful into a greased, hot, heavy pan, running the batter out very thinly so that the flowers form a lacy pattern. Turn and cook the other side. Roll pancakes and serve with orange or lemon juice and melted honey.

ELDERFLOWER CHAMPAGNE

3 heads of elderflower
1 tablesp white wine vinegar
4.8 litres (8 pts) water
7.5 kg (1½ lbs) granulated sugar
1 lemon, squeezed and the peel quartered

Put everything in a large scrupulously clean bowl, cover with clingfilm and leave in a cool place for 48 hours. Strain and bottle in screw-top bottles. Serve chilled with a twist of lemon.
It is is ready to drink in 2 to 3 weeks. If you plan to keep it longer use the champagne-type bottles. Other bottles could explode which is not only dangerous but unbelievably sticky! Do not use plastic mineral water bottles, the base blows into a dome and they fall over. Despite this it is a delicious drink and very easy to make.

ELDERFLOWER CORDIAL   Makes about 3 pts

2 lemons, sliced
20 heads of elderflower
65 g (2½ oz) citric acid
2 kg (4 lbs) sugar
1.5 ltr (2½ pts) water
1 Camden tablet

Heat a cup of the water, the sugar and citric acid over a low light, stir until dissolved.   Boil the rest of the water, pour over lemons and elderflowers, add sugar solution.   Cover with cling film and leave in a cool place for 5 days, stirring twice a day.   Add the Camden tablet, stir in, then strain and bottle.

This cordial will keep for a year or two.   Serve with mineral water and ice...or a drop of gin.

ELDERFLOWER SORBET

9 dl (1½ pts) water
350 g (12 oz) caster sugar
16 elderflower heads
juice of 2 lemons
white of 1 large free-range egg

Put sugar and water in pan and simmer gently until dissolved. Wash elderflowers, shake dry, add to pan and remove from heat. Leave 30 mins to infuse. Strain, add lemon juice, cool, then pour into plastic box and freeze an hour or so until semi-frozen.   Beat egg white until firm but not stiff, fold into sorbet and refreeze.   Serve in wine glasses garnished with crystallised mint leaves.

Freeze plastic bags each containing 16 elderflower heads for winter use.

ELDERFLOWER VINEGAR

elderflowers
wine vinegar

Pack a jar with elderflower heads (shake to remove insects, pull off the coarser stalks) and cover with wine vinegar. Leave in a dark place for three weeks shaking occasionally, then strain and bottle. Use in salad dressings, or a little in a fruit salad.

ELDERFLOWER JELLY

6 large elderflowers
4 tablesp lemon juice
1.75 kg (4 lbs) cooking apples
1.75 ltr (3 pts) water
approx 1 kg (2 lbs) sugar

Wash the apples, do not peel or core, chop them and add to the water in a pan. Bring to boil, simmer about 30 mins until soft. Allow juice to drip through a jelly bag overnight. Allow 1 lb sugar to each pint of juice and bring to boil in a preserving pan adding the elderflowers tied in a muslin bag. Remove this after 5 or 10 minutes, squeezing out the flavoured juice, then boil until setting point is reached (approx 20 minutes).

WILD ROSE
Scatter petals on salads. See section IV for how to crystallise for cake decoration.

IVY LEAVED TOADFLAX
This plant with tiny purple flowers grows on walls. The leaves make an attractive addition to a salad. (Try damping them and sticking to the inner sides of a glass salad bowl.)

PIGNUT

Pignut is a delicate-looking relative of cow parsley, common in fields and woods. Children used to dig down with a penknife to reach the edible nut or tuber (the small brown nut has to be scraped clean) but apart from the novelty of trying out the flavour it would seem a lot of effort for very little food!

MARJORAM (Oregano)

The attractive pinky red flowers are fairly common in the dales (and incidentally dry well for winter decoration). Use same as the cultivated variety to flavour herb butter, soups salads and stews. Roger Phillips quotes a recipe for **Marjoram sugar** - add the chopped flowers and buds to a jar of sugar and stand it in the sun for 24 hours (2 or 3 days?! then sieve I presume) and add to cakes and desserts.

MARJORAM JELLY   (Roger Phillips)

2 kg (4 lb) cooking apples
6 dl (1 pt) water
1½ dl (¼ pt) white vinegar
large bunch marjoram
sugar

Wash apples, chop, put in preserving pan with vinegar, water and three-quarters of the marjoram leaves. Simmer about 45 mins. Strain through jelly bag, do not squeeze if you want a clear jelly. Measure juice and allow 1 lb to 1 pint and make jelly in usual way, adding the remaining leaves finely chopped when setting point is reached. Stir after 5 minutes and pot.

THYME is common on the limestone where it flowers all through the summer. Milder than the cultivated forms. It is is a classic herb for bouquet garni and stuffings.

THYME AND SOUR CREAM DRESSING   (Roger Phillips)

1 dl (4 fl oz) soured cream   **1 tablesp olive oil**
2 tablesp thyme   **pepper and salt**
1 teasp lemon juice   **garlic**

Chop the thyme very finely then mix in a jar with oil, lemon juice and
a little crushed garlic. Shake well then stir into sour cream and add
salt and pepper. A gorgeous dressing for beetroot, cucumber or any
kind of bean salad.

CARAWAY is not commonly found growing
wild in this area, but does so on one fairly
isolated village green. The story goes that a
pedlar woman long ago was selling her wares
when the village boys teased her laden donkey
with a thistle. The donkey kicked and spilt
the contents of his load, which included a bag
of caraway seeds. See section II for seed cake,
and use in goulash.

106

YARROW
Make yarrow tea by infusing fresh or dried leaves.   Add a few chopped leaves to a cream cheese sandwich.

HEATHER should not go without a mention when it clothes our moor tops so magnificently in August, and provides food and shelter for the game birds. There is some mention of heather tops being infused as tea and as a flavouring for beer in Scotland, but not in this area as far as I know. A few people have bee-hives on the moors to produce the deliciously flavoured HEATHER HONEY.

CRACKPOT ROLLS
Slice **granary rolls** twice, horizontally. **Butter** the four cut sides. Spread the bottom slice with **heather honey** and **thin slices of Swaledale cheese.**   Add the middle slice, spread with **peanut butter** then add a **crisp lettuce leaf** and cover with the top slice.
Best assembled and eaten straight away ....
ideally on a sunny late August day on Whitaside, looking over to Crackpot and up the winding Swale!

JUNIPER
Juniper trees are still fairly widespread in Swaledale.   The berries take three years to mature and are then blue/black. You will need old clothes and gloves, the thorns are very prickly. *(In Umbria where they are harvested for gin the farmers use a mesh tray and beat the bush with a stick. You might try an upturned old umbrella under the bush, but for a small quantity I prefer to select the best berries by hand)* Dry the berries on a metal tray preferably outdoors, turning frequently, then store in an airtight jar. I have not come across a recipe for home made gin; but add the crushed berries to game dishes, to bouquets garnis, to cabbage, and to onion soup.

PAPRIKA PORK with JUNIPER and ELDERBERRY

serves 4 to 6

30 g (1½ oz) butter
2 tablesp oil
1.5 kg (3¼ lbs) pork
1 carrot, sliced
1 onion, chopped
1 clove garlic, crushed
1 teasp juniper berries
1½ tablesp paprika
2 tablesp plain flour
5 fl oz elderberry wine
3 fl oz tomato purée
2 bay leaves
2 sprigs fresh thyme
2 sprigs fresh parsley
1.3 ltr (1¼ pts) chicken stock

for glazed onions: **100 g (4 oz) raisins**
4 fl oz (¼ pt) elderberry wine
(or red wine plus a cube or two of frozen elderberry juice)
30 g (1¼ oz) butter
3 medium onions, sliced   2 teasp sugar

Dice pork, crush juniper berries. Heat butter in pan, fry pork in batches until browned. Transfer to casserole. Drain all but 1 tablesp liquid from pan and put in carrot, onion, garlic and juniper. Cook, stirring until soft. Add paprika and flour, cook, stirring until combined.
Remove from heat, stir in wine, purée, herbs and stock, stir until it thickens slightly; pour over pork in casserole. Bake, covered, in a moderate oven for 1 hour or until pork is tender; discard herbs and cool.   Combine raisins and wine in a bowl, cover and leave overnight. Refrigerate pork dish overnight.
Next day skim fat from casserole and re-heat. Serve topped with **glazed onions** - heat butter in pan, add onions and sugar, cook, covered, over low heat about 45 mins. or until onions are lightly browned and very soft.   Add raisins and wine and stir until bubbling.

JUNIPER BERRIES WITH LAMB   (serves 4)

12 lamb cutlets
2 cloves of garlic, sliced
2 teasp dried juniper berries
1 medium carrot, chopped
1 stick celery, chopped
1 medium onion, chopped
1 tablesp fresh rosemary leaves
1 tablesp oil
4 fl oz dry white wine
8 fl oz water
sprig rosemary
1 tablesp plain flour
1 tablesp water (extra)
½ teasp sugar
1 teasp light soy sauce
1 tablesp fresh chopped parsley

Make small cuts in the lamb with a sharp knife. Put a sliver of
garlic, a few leaves of rosemary and a juniper berry into each incision.
Heat oil in flameproof dish, add vegetables and cook , stirring, until
onion is soft. Stir in wine, water and rosemary and add the lamb.
Bake, uncovered, in moderate oven 40-50 mins or until meat is
tender.
Remove cutlets and keep hot; drain juices, (the tasty pulp can be
served, or reserved to add to soup later). Heat 8 fl oz reserved juices,
stir in blended flour and water, soy sauce and sugar. Stir over heat
until sauce thickens, simmer 5 mins then stir in parsley and serve
with the lamb.

BILBERRIES ripen on the moors around August so take care not to be there when there is grouse shooting.
Wonderful in a pie, or add a few to a rather special

SPONGE SUMMER PUDDING

750 g (1½ lbs) mixed soft fruit -
bilberries, raspberries, blackcurrants,
redcurrants, blackberries.
3 heads elderflower (frozen, they will have
finished flowering when the berries are ripe)
100 g (4 oz) caster sugar

for the sponge -
2 eggs, separated
100 g (4 oz) caster sugar
75 g (3 oz) plain flour, sifted

Whisk egg whites until stiff, gradually add yolks and sugar, whisking until mixture is pale fluffy. Fold in the flour, pour into a 20 cm (8 in.) tin and bake at 350ºF 180ºC gas 4 for 20 mins.
Stew the fruit gently until the juices run, add elderflowers and sugar, allow to cool then remove elderflowers, squeezing out the juice.
Line a 1.2 litre (2 pt) bowl with slices of sponge. Ladle in half the fruit and juice, add more sponge slices, then the rest of the fruit and top with a final layer of cake. Put a saucer in the top of the bowl and a 2 lb weight (or a couple of large tins of tomatoes) on that. Chill for several hours. Turn out the pudding and garnish with fresh leaves (sweet cicely or redcurrant). Serve with cream or fromage frais.

BILBERRY AND YOGURT TART   serves 4

450 g (1 lb) bilberries
  (or blackberries, or blackcurrants)
225 g (8 oz) flour   pinch salt
175 g (6 oz) butter   2 teasp caster sugar
1 medium egg yolk   1-2 tablesp water
50 g (2 oz) ground almonds   2 eggs, separated
150 ml (¼ pt) double cream
150 ml (¼ pt) yogurt
1 tablesp lemon juice
100 g (4 oz) caster sugar
1 level tablesp cornflour

Make pastry with the flour, salt and fat in the usual way, adding the egg yolk and 1 tablesp water, then the second spoonful if required. Cover and chill 30 mins. Line a 20 cm (8 in.) loose-bottom flan tin with the pastry. Cover base with ground almonds, then the cleaned fruit.   Bake in a hot oven 425°F 220°C gas 7 for 15 mins then remove, and reduce heat to 375°F 190°C gas 5.

Separate eggs, beat cream, yogurt, egg yolks and sugar together. Whisk egg whites until stiff, stir in cornflour. Fold into mixture and spread over tart. Bake a further 40 to 50 minutes until well-risen and golden brown.

BLACKBERRIES The seeds
are a bit gritty except when
eaten fresh, so make

BRAMBLE SYRUP

1.5 kg (3 lb) blackberries
sugar
5 cloves
5 crushed coriander seeds
half cinnamon stick
1 blade mace
peel of half a lemon
  and half an orange

Simmer the fruit with 150 ml
(¼ pt) water until soft, then press
through a nylon sieve   Measure
liquid and to each 600 ml (1 pt) liquid
add 500 g (1 lb) sugar.   Add the
spices and peel, tied in muslin, and
simmer for 30 mins. Remove the bag
then bottle or freeze the syrup.

BRAMBLE JELLY   (Roger Phillips)

1.8 kg (4 lb) blackberries	**3 dl (½ pt) water**
juice of 2 lemons	**sugar**

The jelly sets better if slightly under-ripe berries are used. Wash
fruit and drain well.   Put in preserving pan with lemon juice and
simmer 1 hour.   Strain through jelly bag but do not squeeze or jelly
will be cloudy. Allow 1 lb sugar to 1 pt juice, heat gently until sugar
dissolves then boil 10 to 15 mins until setting point is reached. If
liked jelly may be spiced with **quarter teaspoon each of ground**
mace, nutmeg and cinnamon.

BLACKBERRY AND YOGURT ICECREAM

350 g (12 oz) blackberries
sugar or honey
1.5 dl (¼ pt) plain yogurt

90 ml (3 fl oz) water
2 eggs, separated

Simmer the blackberries with water until soft, press through a nylon sieve to make a purée, then sweeten to taste with sugar or honey Whisk the egg yolks until smooth and light. Heat the purée until boiling, then pour onto the eggs, whisking all the time. Add the yogurt and whisk again. Put in a freezer tray and freeze until just firm. Break up the mixture and return to a bowl. Whisk until smooth. Beat egg whites until stiff and fold in. Return to the freezing tray and freeze until required.

BLACKBERRY CREAMS

(serves 6 to 8)

700 g (1½ lbs) blackberries
150 g (6 oz) caster sugar
13 g (½ oz) gelatine
45 ml (3 tablesp) water
300 ml (½ pt) double cream
30 ml (2 tablesp) runny honey

4 eggs
juice of half a lemon

Stew berries gently until soft, rub through nylon strainer then add 50 g (2 oz) sugar. Cool. Whisk eggs with rest of sugar in a bowl over a pan of hot water until thick. Soak gelatine in lemon juice and water, dissolve over gentle heat. Lightly whip the cream. Add honey and egg-sugar mixture to the purée. Fold in cream with metal spoon until blended. Pour into wine glasses or a large bowl and chill. Serve with shortbread biscuits.

BLACKBERRY WATER ICE

(serves 4)

450 g (1 lb) blackberries
1.5 dl (¼ pt) water

100 g (4 oz) sugar
1 egg white

Boil the sugar and water for a few minutes. Cool. Liquidise the blackberries then press through a sieve and mix with the syrup. Freeze until mushy. Beat egg white until it forms soft peaks, fold into fruit and refreeze. Remove once again from the freezer and stir until light and fluffy. Freeze until required.

BLACKBERRY PANCAKES

225 g (8 oz) blackberries
1 tablesp honey
100 g (4 oz) flour
pinch of salt
2 eggs
2 tablesp melted butter

2 scented geranium leaves
3 tablesp clotted cream
   or fresh cream cheese
1 teasp caster sugar
300 ml (½ pt) milk

Make a syrup by simmering honey in water for 10 mins. Add
blackberries and geranium leaves and poach gently until tender.
Cool. Remove leaves. Strain fruit from syrup and mix with cream
cheese. Make pancakes as with ELDERFLOWER PANCAKES,
roll around the cheese mixture and serve with the scented syrup.

BLACKBERRY AND APPLE ICECREAM

225 g (8 oz) blackberries
900 g (2 lbs) baking apples
2 tablesp lemon juice
150 g (5 oz) caster sugar
300 ml (10 fl oz) yogurt
150 ml (5 fl oz) double cream

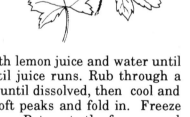

Peel, core and chop the apples, cook with lemon juice and water until
soft. Add blackberries and cook until juice runs. Rub through a
sieve, add the sugar and reheat gently until dissolved, then cool and
chill. Stir in yogurt, whip cream to soft peaks and fold in. Freeze
until firm, remove and beat the icecream. Return to the freezer, and
beat again after a further hour.

HAWTHORN (see also May Blossom)
HAW JELLY   (Roger Phillips)

1 kg (2.2 lb) hawthorn berries   juice of 1 lemon
6 dl (1pt) water   sugar

Clean all the stalks from the berries and put them in a pan with the water and lemon juice. Bring to the boil and then simmer for 45 mins, stirring from time to time. Strain the pulp through a jelly bag overnight. Discard the pulp and measure the juice - for every 6 dl (1pt) add 450 g (1 lb) sugar - and heat gently until the sugar has melted and then until it comes to the boil. Continue to boil rapidly until a really firm setting point is reached (test on a saucer that has been in the freezer. Pour jelly into small moulds such as an ice-cube maker and leave to set. The end result is a stiff, delicately flavoured jelly that can be cut with a knife and served with coffee after dinner. *(Or boil until setting point is reached and pot as with other jellies)*

HAW   SAUCE   (Margaret Hopper)

675 g (1½ lbs) haw berries
100 g (4 oz) sugar   25 g (1 oz) salt
3 gills vinegar   ½ teasp white pepper

Gather the haw berries dry. Wash well, put in preserving pan with vinegar and cook over gentle heat for 30 mins. Press through a sieve. Return to the pan with sugar, salt and pepper and boil for 10 mins. Pour into small pots and seal. This sauce keeps splendidly. *(Note- A Yorkshire gill is half a pint)*

ELDERBERRY CORDIAL   (Margaret Hopper)

Berries must be ripe but not over-ripe. Gather on a dry day, remove stalks, put berries in jars. Stand jars in boiling water until the juice runs. Strain off the juice and to every quart add **1 oz bruised whole ginger, 1 teasp cloves, 2 lbs sugar.** Simmer gently 1 hour, leave until cold. Strain through muslin and bottle.

FROZEN ELDERBERRY JUICE

Gently heat elderberries until the juice runs, then strain, and pour into ice-cube trays. Use in casseroles (such as the pork and juniper dish) or add to a mixed berry purée.

ELDERBERRY PICKLE (Roger Phillips)

675 g (1½ lbs) elderberries (without stems)
50 g (2 oz) light, soft sugar
12 g (½ oz) ground ginger
¼ teasp ground black pepper
pinch ground cloves
3 dl (½ pt) cider vinegar
pinch ground mace
50 g (2 oz) seedless raisins
1 medium onion   1 teasp salt

Wash elderberries very well and drain thoroughly. Sieve the berries, pressing out all the juice, to make a thin purée. Put in a pan with the finely chopped onion and other ingredients. Bring to the boil and then simmer, stirring well, for 20 mins. Pot in small sterilised jars with vinegar-proof lids.

ELDERBERRY RASPBERRY AND REDCURRANT SAUCE

elderberries, raspberries, redcurrants,
sugar to taste, cornflour.
A good way to use a few odd berries. Quantities are a matter of
guesswork! Gently heat the fruit until juices run, rub through a
sieve, return to the pan and sweeten to taste. Mix a dessertsp
cornflour with a little water then add to the hot juices and boil until
thickened. Chill.
Pour a swirl over Greek yogurt and 'feather' a pattern with a skewer.
Or serve over icecream.

Janet Rawlins

ELDERBERRY AND APPLE JELLY   (Roger Phillips)

1.3 kg (3 lb) cooking apples
2.2 ltr (4 pts) elderberries
1.2 ltr (2 pts) water   sugar
peel of an orange and half a stick of cinnamon,
tied together with cotton

See Elderflower jelly for method.

HEDGEROW 'CHEESE'

500 g (1 lb) crab apples   **500 g (1 lb) elderberries**
500 g (1 lb) blackberries   **100 g (4 oz) haws**
225 g (8 oz) sloes   **sugar**

Add the washed fruit to 1.5 litres (3 pts water) and simmer until soft.   Press the pulp through a sieve and discard the skins, stones and pips.   Weigh the pulp and allow 450 g (1 lb) sugar to each 450 g (1 lb) pulp. Return the fruit to the preserving pan, add the sugar and heat gently until it has completely dissolved. Boil until setting point is reached. Pour into warm jars and cover while hot.

MUSHROOMS are easily recognised. Other fungi need the help of a good book or an experienced collector, so I have not included recipes for them.

MUSHROOM AND HAZELNUT PATÉ

50 g (2 oz) butter   1 medium onion, chopped
450 g (1 lb) field mushrooms, chopped
¼ teasp grated nutmeg
grated rind of half lemon   salt & pepper
100 g (4 oz) brown breadcrumbs
50 g (2 oz) hazelnuts, toasted and chopped

Gently cook the onion in the butter until softening, add mushrooms and stew gently for 5 minutes. Whizz in food processor with the other ingredients.   Do not over-process, the paté should not be too smooth. Put into an oiled and lined 450 g (1 lb) loaf tin (or individual ramekins) and refrigerate until firm.

HORSE MUSHROOM CROUSTÂDE   (Roger Phillips)

Croustâde:

100 g (4 oz) soft breadcrumbs
100 g (4 oz) ground almonds or other nuts
50 g (2 oz) butter
100 g (4 oz) flaked almonds or hazelnuts
1 clove garlic, crushed
½ teaspoon mixed herbs

Topping:

450 g (1 lb) mushrooms
50 g (2 oz) butter
2 heaped teasp flour
4.5 dl (¾ pt) milk
salt pepper and nutmeg
4 tomatoes
1 teasp chopped parsley

Croustâde: Mix together breadcrumbs and ground nuts and rub in butter, cut into small pieces. Add flaked almonds, garlic and herbs. Mix together well and press down into an ovenproof dish, making a layer about 1.5 cm (half inch) thick. Bake at 230ºC 450ºF gas 8 for 15 - 17 mins until golden brown.
Topping: Wash and slice the mushrooms, sauté in butter until tender, add flour and when it froths remove from heat and stir in milk.   Return to heat, stir until thickened, then season. Spoon mixture on top of croustâde, top with skinned and sliced tomatoes and a little salt, pepper and nutmeg.   Return to oven for 10 - 15 mins. Serve decorated with parsley.

ROSE HIPS Contain more Vitamin C than any other fruit.

ROSE HIP SYRUP

1350 g (3 lbs) rose hips
675 g (1½ lbs) granulated sugar

Wash the hips and mince, or whizz in a food processor. Add to 2.7 litres (4½ pts) fast boiling water. Bring back to the boil, cover and remove from heat, infuse 15 mins. Strain through several layers of butter-muslin to remove all the whiskers.
Boil the pulp again with another 1.2 litres (2 pts) water   Cover and infuse as before, but leave to drip for an hour or two. Fast boil the strained juices from both batches until reduced to 1.4 litres (2¼ pints).   Dissolve the warmed sugar gently in the juice then boil for 5 mins.   Pour into small, clean, warm bottles, or for long-term storage fill into plastic cartons and freeze. Defrost and decant into bottles as required.
Dilute with mineral water and a squeeze of lemon as a delicious winter drink, or use neat as a sauce on icecreams or pancakes.

ROSE HIP JELLY

1½ kg (3 lb) rose hips
lemon juice
sugar

Simmer the hips in water to cover. Mash, then strain through a fine jelly bag overnight. To each 600 ml (1 pint) juice add the juice of a lemon and 400 g (14 oz) sugar. Stir to dissolve, boil to setting point. Pour into warmed jars, cover.

ROWAN (MOUNTAIN ASH)
Fairly widespread in the
dales, with brilliant scarlet
berries which make a sharp

ROWAN BERRY AND CRAB-APPLE JELLY

(Margaret Hopper)

4 lbs crab apples
2 lbs rowan berries
3 pts water

Cook gently until tender, then strain.
Allow 1 lb sugar to each pint of juice.
Bring slowly to boil then boil rapidly
until setting point is reached. Pot in
small jars and cover whilst hot.
Delicious with any cold meat.

HAZEL trees still remain fairly common, part of the ancient
woodland that clothed the valley sides. In the past the nuts were
harvested in sufficient quantity to sell at markets.

HAZELNUT SOUP

50 g (2 oz) hazelnuts	**2 tablesp butter or oil**
1 small onion	**6 dl (1 pt) milk**
2 teasp flour	**salt, black pepper**

4 tablesp cream or soured cream
chopped parsley or chives
2 sticks celery, chopped

Toast hazelnuts then rub in a cloth to remove skins.   Grind until
powdered.
Heat 1 tablesp butter or oil and sweat the onion (finely chopped) and
celery for a few minutes. Add ground hazelnuts and milk, bring to
boil then simmer very gently for half an hour.
Blend until smooth.   Melt rest of butter or oil, stir in flour and cook a
minute or so. Gradually add the soup, stirring, and cook 4 minutes.
Season. Garnish with the cream and herbs.

121

HAZELNUT MERINGUE   (serves 6)
(Roger Phillips from Mary Norvak)

75 g (3 oz) hazelnuts
75 g (3 oz) ground almonds   6 egg whites
3 dl (½ pint) double cream   icing sugar
350 g (12 oz) caster sugar   fresh or frozen fruit

Chop the hazelnuts finely, preferably in a blender, and mix well with the almonds. Whisk the egg whites to stiff peaks. Add half the sugar and whisk again until the mixture is stiff and shiny. Fold in the remaining sugar and nuts. Brush three 25 cm (9 in) sandwich tins lightly with oil and line with circles of baking parchment. Brush the lining paper with oil. Put the mixture in the tins and spread lightly with a spatula to the edges of the tin. Bake at 170°C 325°F gas 3 for 45 mins. Leave in tins for 5 mins, then turn onto cooling racks, carefully removing paper from bases. Leave until cold.
Whip cream stiffly. Assemble layers of meringue with cream and chosen fruit between. Dust the top thickly with icing sugar.

SLOES (the fruit of the Blackthorn)

Make **SLOE GIN** from **sloes, sugar and gin.** The bitter black fruit should be left on the trees until after a frost or two. This also makes them easier to see, when some of the leaves have dropped. *(Take a stick for hooking down the branches and wear old clothes, the thorns are sharp!)*
Wash the sloes and spread out on kitchen paper and newspaper to dry, then settle down with your favourite TV programme and a silver or stainless steel fork *(I use a tiny corn-cob holder).* Prick each sloe and put them into large jars (instant coffee jars are ideal).
Fill up the jars with gin, then pour over sugar until it comes a quarter to a third of the way up the jar. Keep in a dark place, shake occasionally and top up with gin as the fruit shrinks. Taste, and add more sugar if required. It will be ready to strain and bottle by Christmas.
*Don't throw away the gin-soaked sloes, if you can be bothered to scrape the flesh off the fairly large stones. (Another satisfying TV-watching job!) Add to crumbled Wensleydale cheese and blend until smooth to make a delicious **rosy spread for canapés***

SLOE JELLY   (Roger Phillips, from Jenny Stone)

2 kg (4 lb) sloes   6 dl (1 pt) water   2 kg (4 lbs) sugar

Pick sloes when fully ripe. Wash well and get rid of any bits of leaves. Put into pressure cooker and cook with 6 dl (1 pt) water for 5 mins at high pressure - or in open pan about 40 mins. Pour into jelly bag and allow liquid to drip through overnight. Warm sugar then add to fruity juice. Boil until it reaches setting point, which takes about half an hour or so.

(Alternatively use 3 lbs sloes and 1 lb crab apples and add a cinnamon stick, a blade of mace, 10 cloves and 6 allspice berries to make a **SPICED JELLY**.)

SLOE CHUTNEY   (Margaret Hopper)

6 lbs sloes or bullaces or mixture of both
2 pts spiced vinegar   1½ lbs sugar
1 salt spoon ground ginger   1 salt spoon cayenne pepper
1 teasp powdered allspice   1 oz salt

Cook the fruit in the vinegar until tender. Cool, then remove stones. Add the rest of the ingredients and cook slowly until a suitable consistency. All chutney is best if cooked for a long time very slowly. Pot and cover whilst hot.

123

SECTION IV
FOOD FOR TODAY

Changes such as refrigerators freezers, microwaves, food processors and supermarkets have revolutionised our eating patterns. One hears complaints that families no longer eat together; of 'grazing'; fast food; junk food; convenience food; eating with one eye on the television. Much of it unavoidable with today's lifestyles perhaps, but in contrast there is a growing interest in wholefoods, vegetarianism, herbs and a healthy diet.

Increased travel has made us more adventurous in our tastes. In the old days rice meant pudding, and beans meant you-know-who. It is only in the past ten years or so that I have become familiar with the numerous pulses and pastas that are now available - thankfully most local markets have wholefood stalls.

Many village shops have disappeared as more people travel further afield. Those that remain are greatly appreciated and well supported, and we also have a number of travelling shops (even fish & chips!). However, the selection, especially of vegetables, has to be limited, and most of us combine an occasional day out with a chance to stock-up in one of the big supermarkets. Then various dishes can be prepared and stashed away in the freezer along with fruit and herbs from the garden and the countryside. It is only occasionally that we find we are at any disadvantage, and we do have the benefit of milk, cream and free-range eggs from local farms.

ENTERTAINING

Entertaining at home can include everything from old friends turning up just before lunch (one of the joys - or hazards - of living in a lovely part of the country), young families coming home for a week or so, picnics, buffet parties or dinner parties. There are suggestions for all these in the following pages.

SHOWS, PARTIES AND FUND-RAISING EVENTS

The Upper Dales have a thriving social life. These small communities support numerous charities and I am continually impressed by the generosity of people who produce magnificent cakes for the cake stalls and then attend the events in order to buy one made by somebody else!

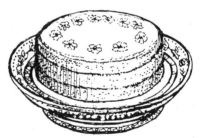

A CAKE FOR THE CAKE STALL - LEMON SANDWICH

100 g (4 oz) s.r. flour **100 g (4 oz) butter or marge**
2 eggs **4 oz caster sugar**
finely grated lemon rind **salt**

Beat sugar and butter until fluffy, slowly add egg and lemon rind, then fold in flour. Have ready 2 greased and lined sandwich tins, divide mixture between them, spread level and bake in centre of mod oven 180ºC 350ºF Gas 4 for 20-25 mins.
Make a butter cream filling with 1½ oz butter, 3 oz icing sugar. Make an icing for the top with 3 oz sieved icing sugar added to warmed lemon juice.

The annual Red Cross Association Punch and Paté Supper in Askrigg has signalled the start of our winter season (when most of the tourists and visiting families have left) for many years. Always an impressive sight with game patés, vegetarian patés and numerous cheeses. Min Tallantire was the group leader for 22 years.

SIMPLE GROUSE PATÉ   Min Tallantire

1 brace mature grouse   salt, pepper
1 small onion, chopped   a little ground mace
4 oz butter
1 slice bread without crust
(optional extra - a small glass of port, madeira or brandy)
Pressure cook grouse with onion - or cook slowly with added stock in the oven for 2½ hours until tender. Skin, and remove bones - then pass through a fine mincer, twice. Work in softened butter and breadcrumbs, adding a little strained stock to moisten. Season with salt and pepper and a little ground mace. Press the mixture into a shallow dish. To keep - seal with clarified butter.

Min's CHRISTMAS RELISH (Piccalilli)
is legendary, she has made it "by the ton" over the years, and has now decided to retire from the mammoth boil-ups and part with her recipe.

2 large cauliflower (yielding about 2 lbs)
2 lbs onions   2 lbs green tomatoes
2½ lbs sugar   ½ oz turmeric
¼ lb mustard powder   ½ lb salt
1 quart white vinegar   4 oz flour

Use a stainless steel pan if possible.
(1) Prepare vegetables and cut into small pieces. Place in a large bowl with 4 quarts of cold water and sprinkle on half lb salt. Mix well and leave to stand overnight. Next day put all into a large pan and bring to the boil, cook for approx 5 minutes. Remove from heat and strain vegetables in a colander. (2) Boil vinegar and sugar - make a paste of the flour, mustard and turmeric (adding water to mix). Stir some of the boiled vinegar into this mixture, whisking to keep it smooth - then gradually add to the pan of boiling vinegar. Bring all to the boil again and cook for 2 - 3 minutes. Add the drained vegetables and bring back to the boil, stirring well, for another 5 minutes. Leave to cool and pot into jars with screw tops.

POTTED BLUE WENSLEYDALE

450 g (1 lb) blue Wensleydale cheese
225 g (8 oz) unsalted butter
small glass port

Food processors certainly take the hassle out of things like this...just whizz all together. Otherwise, grate the cheese and gradually beat in the butter and then the port. Spoon into small pots, cover. (Can be frozen.)

For a more economical (and slightly less calorific) version to eat in a day or two, use white Wensleydale cheese, adding red wine and yogurt until the desired consistency is reached. It stiffens up quite a lot in the fridge.

The following contributions are from Anne Middleton of Skelgill, who is a regular prizewinner in the cookery section at Askrigg Show. She says they are good tray-bakes to cut and carry for children's parties, picnics, or tea in the field at hay or silage time. They keep well, but I doubt if they get the chance with three young Middletons helping!

PANDORA SLICES
Line a large Swiss-roll tin (8" by 12") with shortcrust pastry and cover with red jam.

4 oz margarine   **4 oz mixed dried fruit**
4 oz sugar   **2 oz walnuts (broken)**
2 eggs   **2 oz cherries, chopped**
4 oz s.r. flour   **1 tablesp sugar**
1 lemon

Grate lemon rind. Cream together marge and sugar. Mix in eggs and fold in flour. Add lemon rind, mixed fruit, walnuts and cherries. Mix well and spread over pastry. Bake at 180ºC/ 350ºF for 45 mins. Mix squeezed lemon juice with the tablesp sugar and spoon over cooked mixture. Return to oven and cook for a few more minutes. When cool cut into squares or slices.

Anne Middleton

FLAPJACK

6 oz margarine
6 oz porridge oats
4 oz sugar
2 oz s.r. flour
pinch of salt
optional - coconut
dried fruit
chopped nuts
cooking chocolate

Melt together the marge and sugar, then mix in other ingredients. Add any of the optional ingredients if you wish. Press into a deep tin and bake at 190ºC 375ºF for 20 - 30 mins until golden. Spread with melted chocolate while still warm. (Half of mixture fits nicely into a sandwich tin.)

SAUSAGE PLAIT   serves 6

1 lb pork sausage meat
4 oz gammon or bacon, sliced
1 onion, finely chopped
2 oz carrots, finely grated
1 level tablesp fresh chopped parsley
optional - 2 oz breadcrumbs

1 egg, beaten
salt & pepper
Worcestershire sauce
8 oz frozen pastry, thawed

Set oven to 220ºC 425ºF gas 7, Put all ingredients for filling into a bowl with half the egg and mix well. Roll out pastry to 12" by 7". Shape meat to a fat 7" sausage and put in middle of pastry. Make diagonal cuts down each side of the pastry and 'plait' these over the top of the meat, securing with some beaten egg if necessary. Put on a baking sheet and brush with beaten egg.   Bake for 20 mins, then reduce temperature to 200ºC 400ºF gas 6 and cook for a further 20 - 25 minutes. Cover with foil if getting too brown. Serve hot or cold.

Anne Middleton

From family picnics to a luxury *CELEBRATION HAMPER* (for four) devised by Maureen Hindes, which was awarded the Yorkshire Countrywomen's Association silver cup.

CANTALOUPE CUPS WITH GINGER SAUCE

2 cantaloupe melons	**half a pineapple**
2 kiwi fruit	**green seedless grapes**

Cut the melons in half with a zig zag edge, cut flesh with a melon baller. Peel and cube the pineapple.

Sauce: **3 pieces of preserved ginger, grated**
1 heaped tablesp ginger marmalade
quarter pint each of double cream and fromage frais
4 tablesp Advocaat

Whisk fromage frais and cream, add the rest and mix well.
Pile the fruit into the hollowed out shells and serve with the sauce.

WENSLEYDALE CHICKEN SUPREME

4 chicken supremes (boneless breasts) with skin on.	
half a medium onion	**4 oz chopped cooked spinach**
4 oz Wensleydale cheese	**1 tablesp chopped parsley**
1 tablesp fine breadcrumbs	**half a beaten egg**
salt, pepper and grated nutmeg	

Finely chop onion and sauté in butter until soft. Finely chop the cheese, then mix all stuffing ingredients together.
Place each chicken breast skin side up on a board, loosen skin and stuff a quarter of the filling under each one. Tuck the skin and meat under the breast to form an even, round dome shape. Put in a buttered baking dish and bake at 180ºC 350ºF gas 4 for 30-35 minutes until golden brown.
Serve cold, sliced into 4, with watercress and tiny tomatoes.

RICE, PRAWN AND ALMOND SALAD

1 large onion	**4 oz shelled prawns**
4 oz cooked long-grain rice	**2 oz almonds**
⅛ pint french dressing	

Finely chop onion and cook in 1 tablesp oil. Blanch, flake, and toast almonds until light brown. Mix ingredients, garnishing with the almonds.

BUCKS FIZZ Dissolve 1 tablesp **sugar** in 2 tablesp **water,** add the juice from **10 large oranges, 1-2 tablesp Grand Marnier.** Chill. Half fill wine glasses, and top up with **champagne.**

Maureen's basket included a **YORKSHIRE CURD TART,** so here is a West Yorkshire variation of the cheesecake.

Take **8 oz shortcrust pastry,** made from the following recipe

> **16 oz plain flour   4 oz lard**
> **6 oz butter and marge mixed**
> **8 tablesp cold water**
> **pinch of salt**

Filling:

8 oz curd cheese   **4 oz butter**
4 oz sugar   **1 egg**
1 tablesp currants   **rum, or nutmeg**
                          Mixed lightly with a fork

Line an 8" or 10" tin with the pastry and bake blind for 10 mins, then add filling and bake until golden brown, 20-30 mins at 425ºF

EATING OUT

As the popularity of the Dales has increased so have the number and variety of hotels, guest houses, restaurants, bed-and-breakfasts and pub bar meals. Dining out may still be only an occasional treat for most of us, but there is now a considerable choice of venues. A few of their talented cooks have very kindly contributed recipes to this section.

At the tiny **Rowan Tree** *restaurant in Askrigg Derek and Pia Wylie are achieving a national reputation. Gourmets travel from far afield to enjoy their delectable food . Derek is from Ireland, Pia from Germany.*

CHOWDER PROVENÇAL   serves 4

1 onion, coarsely chopped	1 tablesp olive oil
500 g (1 lb) potatoes	1 fish stock cube

150 mls (¼ pt) semi-skimmed milk
1 sprig fresh thyme
600 g (1¼ lbs) smoked cod fillet
1 small can sweetcorn kernels, drained
1 small can tomatoes, drained and chopped
4 tablesp single cream
100 mls (4 fl oz) dry white wine
freshly ground black pepper

In a large heavy pan brown the onion in 1 tablesp oil. Peel and chop the potatoes and put into the pan with 1 pt of water, adding fish stock cube, milk and thyme. Bring to boil then simmer for approx. 20 mins until the potato chunks are barely tender. Skin and bone the fish and cut into about 12 chunks and add to the pan with the sweetcorn and tomato. Cover and cook for 5 minutes.

For the garnish:

1 garlic clove, peeled and halved	
8-12 small slices French bread	
75 g (3 oz) prawns	2 tablesp chopped parsley
pinch of saffron	2 tablesp olive oil

Rub the slices of bread with the garlic, sprinkle it with 1 tablesp olive oil and toast both sides under the grill. Rub a small pan with more garlic, add 1 tablesp oil, the prawns and saffron and heat through.   Before serving the chowder stir in the cream and white wine. Season, then ladle into heated soup bowls. Garnish with prawns and sprinkle on parsley.   Serve with the garlic-flavoured croutons.   The addition of about 100 g (4 oz) of thick cut smoked bacon after browning the onions makes the chowder into a robust one-pot meal.   (Derek Wylie)

GRILLED LAMB WITH BEETROOT ORANGE CONFIT
serves 4

4 chump chops, each about 250 g (8 oz)
1 kg (2¼ lbs) beetroot
50 g (2 oz) butter
300 mls (½ pt) orange juice
2 tablesp finely grated orange zest
1 teasp freshly chopped thyme leaves
150 mls (¼ pt) raspberry vinegar
sugar to taste   salt and pepper

Wash and peel the beetroot. Cut into fine julienne strips. Melt butter, add beetroot and sweat gently. Pour in orange juice and add zest, thyme and vinegar. Simmer uncovered for 30 mins stirring occasionally until beetroot is tender and mixture is thick and resembles jam. Taste and adjust seasoning with sugar, salt and pepper.   Meanwhile place chops under a hot grill and cook for 10 mins on each side. Transfer to a warm plate and add a spoonful of confit. Serve with a selection of vegetables and potatoes.

(Derek Wylie)

SATAY STYLE MARINADE FOR PORK CUTLETS

serves 6

6 generous sized pork chops with the kidney on
5 tablesp peanut butter
300 ml (½ pt) coconut milk
1 tablesp soft brown sugar   **2 tablesp soy sauce**

Mix ingredients thoroughly in a small bowl. Pour over chops and leave to marinate. To cook, heat oven to 180°C 350°F gas 4. Lightly butter a piece of foil and wrap the chops in this, with a little of the marinade. One-third fill a roasting tin with hot water, put in a wire rack and lay the foil parcel on this. Cook for 30 mins. Remove chops from foil and keep warm. Carefully pour the juices from the foil into a pan along with the remaining marinade and reduce.
Make a cream sauce with:

425 mls (¾ pt) double cream
1 teasp salt   **1 tablesp chutney**

Put cream and salt in a fairly wide heavy based pan and place over half your lit hob. Add the reduced marinade. In 20 minutes beat in the chutney and your sauce is ready.

(Derek Wylie)

ATHOLL BROSE

3 - 4 tablesp honey   **4 tablesp whisky**
2 tablesp oatmeal   **300 ml (½ pt) double cream**

Heat honey and whisky until just dissolved, then leave to cool slightly. Toast the oatmeal gently in a dry frying pan. Whisk the cream until thick but not completely stiff. Sprinkle with most of the oatmeal, reserving 2 teasp. Fold the oatmeal, honey and whisky into the cream and divide between 4 whisky tumblers. Sprinkle with the remaining oatmeal and chill until needed.   (Derek Wylie)

Pat and Robin West run the delightful 17th century (and earlier) **Countersett Hall** *near Semerwater as a guest house. For a few weeks each year they open as the Midwinter Restaurant when we locals are able to enjoy Pat's inspired dishes.*

Pat says "Without being too adventurous I like to make 'ordinary food' more interesting, and as something of a scatterbrained cook - often not deciding on the menu until the last minute - I happen on some very tasty surprises! Time is always at a premium, and living so far away from suppliers, making do with what is in stock becomes something of a challenge. My recipes are all results of these criteria"

AVOCADO AND STRAWBERRY MOUSSE   serves 6

2 large ripe avocado pears *(it's fine if they are not perfect)*
1 pkt cream cheese
2 oz softened butter
1 teasp Dijon - or any mild mustard
a pinch of salt,
a good few turns of ground black pepper
and a squeeze of lemon
4 oz chopped strawberries
Peel and stone the avocados, liquidise all ingredients except strawberries until smooth, then stir in the strawberries. Cover closely with cling film and chill for 30 mins. Serve a neat dollop of this, sprinkled with more black pepper, with a small salad and Melba toast or toast fingers.   (Pat West)

135

TROUT AND SALMON PIE   serves 6

2½ lbs of salmon, trout, prawns, in any combination,
cut into large chunks with all skin and bones removed
1 tin cut asparagus   10 fl oz milk
15 fl oz cream (double if poss.)
1 heaped tablesp cornflour and a drop of water
salt and pepper   1 tablesp dried parsley

Poach the fish in the milk with the salt and pepper in a large
saucepan for about 20 mins.   Carefully scoop the fish into a large
casserole dish, leaving the liquid in the pan. Drain the liquid from
the asparagus into the saucepan, putting asparagus cuts into dish
with fish. Mix cornflour with water and add to cream.   Bring fish
liquid to boil and stir in cream. Cook, stirring for a few minutes,
then pour over the fish.   Cover with one of the following toppings and
bake 400ºF 200ºC for about 25 - 30 min until golden.

Topping 1.   2 lb potato mashed with butter and a tablesp yogurt.
Topping 2.   Layers of filo pastry, each layer brushed with melted
butter.   (Pat West)

PAT'S BREAD AND BUTTER PUDDING   serves 6

4 slices of bread, buttered on both sides and cut diagonally
into quarters
3 or 4 tablesp Amaretto or Marsala
1 tin apricot pie filling   1 heaped tablesp raisins
2 heaped tablesp sugar   1 teasp vanilla essence
1 pt single cream   3 eggs size 1 (or 4 smaller)
a small handful of flaked almonds

Put half of the bread in the bottom of a casserole dish, big enough to
take the bread in a single layer. Sprinkle with half the sugar, half
the raisins or sultanas and all of the booze.   Spread the apricot on
top and sprinkle with the remaining dried fruit.   Arrange the rest of
the bread on top, overlapping the slices to leave the corners showing.
Beat the eggs with the remaining sugar, the vanilla essence and the
cream.   Pour this over the bread and leave to soak for 30 mins.
Sprinkle the almonds on top and bake, 190ºC 375ºF, for 45 mins or
until the top is brown and the middle is softly set.

                                            (Pat West)

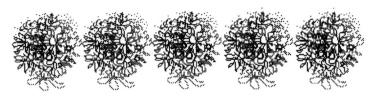

Here are three examples of the imaginative dishes Margaret Baker provides in her charming small guest house,
West Lea Askrigg.

WENSLEYDALE MUSHROOMS   serves 6
Wensleydale cheese melts to a delicious nuttiness

2 rashers smoked bacon   6 oz small mushrooms
37 g (1½ oz) butter   37 g (1½ oz) plain flour
2.1 dl (⅓ pt) milk
100 g (4 oz) grated Wensleydale cheese
salt & pepper to taste   ½ teasp made English mustard

Chop mushrooms and fry gently in butter - do not brown. Add the bacon, de-rinded and chopped in small pieces. Cook for 2 to 3 mins until sizzling but not browned. Remove from heat, add flour, stir well, add milk and return to heat. Bring to boil, cook very gently until thickened, adding a little more milk if necessary. Add 3 oz of the cheese, and the mustard, salt & pepper. Place in 6 buttered ramekins, sprinkle with remaining cheese and bake or grill until bubbling and brown.
Will serve 4 for a light lunch with salad.   (Margaret Baker)

PARSNIP AND CELERIAC SOUP   serves 6
A glorious warming soup, pale, thick and creamy.

1.2 litres (2 pts) strong chicken stock
2 large parsnips   2 large potatoes
1 root celeriac (about 1 lb)
2 large onions   75 g (3 oz) butter

to serve - **4.5 dl (¾ pt) milk**
1.5 dl (¼ pt) single cream
1 tablesp chopped parsley
seasoning

Peel and chop the onions. Peel and chop root vegetables into medium -sized pieces. Fry onions gently in butter until softened but not browned. Add other vegetables and cook briefly to coat pieces in

137

the butter. Add chicken stock, bring to the boil and simmer 45 mins or until celeriac is softened. Allow to cool. Liquidise until smooth, or mash with a potato masher for a less smooth soup. Check seasoning.

Before serving bring to the boil, add milk, reheat but do *not* ~~do~~ reboil. Serve in a hot tureen with cream and parsley added at the last minute.

(Margaret Baker)

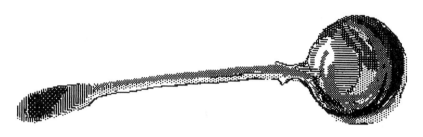

MULLED FRUIT SALAD   serves 6
A lovely pudding for Christmas and a way of using up any left-over red wine

**1 tin best quality pitted black cherries
3 large English Conference pears
3 large juicy oranges
rind of a large lemon
3 dl (½ pt) red wine or perhaps
1.5 dl (¼ pt) port wine + same of water
100 g (4 oz) sugar
1 stick cinnamon
4 cloves
1 piece root ginger**

Prepare syrup by placing sugar, wine and lemon rind and spices in a heavy pan. Heat gently until sugar is dissolved. *Do not boil.* Allow to infuse for at least 2 hrs, or overnight. Meanwhile peel and quarter the pears and poach in 1.5 dl (¼ pt.) water until just tender, Allow to cool. Peel oranges and cut into slices. Strain the mulled wine into a large serving bowl, add the drained pears, sliced oranges and the tin of cherries. Serve with thick double cream and home-made shortbread.

(Margaret Baker)

Owen Metcalfe's **Crown Inn** *at Askrigg, Wensleydale,*
generally referred to just as as "Owen's", is a genuine local-family-run
'local', (recently sympathetically re-furbished) where you can enjoy the
best of home cooking. With their delicious roast ham comes this tasty
chutney:

GREEN TOMATO CHUTNEY

2 lb green tomatoes
1 lb cooking apples
1 lb onions or shallots
12 oz mixed seedless raisins
        & chopped dates
12 oz soft brown sugar
20 g tub of pickling spice
1 teasp salt
¾ pt malt vinegar

Put the chopped tomatoes, apples and onions in a heavy based pan
with half the vinegar, bring to the boil, then simmer gently until
tender. Tie the pickling spice in a muslin bag and add to the pan
with the raisins and dates. Cook, stirring from time to time until the
mixture thickens after about 1 hour. Add the salt, sugar and the
rest of the vinegar, stirring until the sugar dissolves. Continue
cooking, squeezing the spice bag occasionally with a wooden spoon
until the mixture is thick. Remove the spice bag before potting and
sealing in sterilised jars. Leave to mature at least 6 weeks.

(Owen Metcalfe)

139

The Fox and Hounds at Starbotton in Wharfedale offers a tempting menu with traditional - plus adventurous vegetarian - dishes, and superb Yorkshire pudding! Jimmy and Hilary McFadyen came from Scotland in 1991 and have already won an Egon Ronay award for 'best newcomers'. Here are two of Hilary's wicked puddings:

CLOOTIE DUMPLING (A traditional Scottish pudding) serves 16

1 lb self-raising flour
8 oz currants
8 oz raisins
1 teasp ginger
2 eggs
¼ pt milk (to mix)
½ teasp bicarb. soda

12 oz sultanas
8 oz dark brown sugar
1 teasp cinnamon
1 teasp mixed spice
8 oz suet
4 oz breadcrumbs

Place all dry ingredients in a bowl, mix well, then add eggs and enough milk to make a solid dough. Flour a pudding cloth ('cloot'), place dough in centre, tie tightly leaving a little room for expansion. Place in a pan of boiling water for 4 hours. Carefully unwrap cloth and serve hot with custard. (Hilary McFadyen)

MISSISSIPPI MUD PIE   serves 12

12 oz chocolate digestive biscuits
4 oz butter
5 tablesp milk
1 pt double cream

12 oz marshmallows
15 oz plain chocolate

Melt butter, add to crushed biscuits and line a 10 inch round tin, base and sides. Melt the marshmallows in the milk, cool a little then add melted chocolate and the whipped cream. Stir until smooth and pour over biscuit base. Refrigerate for 4 hours, decorate with piped cream. (Hilary McFadyen)

And for something more down to earth, hot for a quickie lunch or cold for a picnic -

CHEGONATO CRUSTIES   serves 4

4 granary rolls   **butter**
6 eggs   **4 tomatoes**
half an onion (optional)
75 g (3 oz) grated Wensleydale cheese
salt and freshly ground black pepper

Cut off the tops of the rolls, removing a conical 'plug'.   Butter the lids, and the tops and hollows of the rolls.   Bake or grill until crisp and brown.
Finely chop the onion and fry in a nut of butter in a saucepan until soft but not brown.   Pour boiling water over the tomatoes, then peel and chop. Add to the onion (if using), cook in a little butter until most of the liquid has evaporated.   Add the lightly beaten eggs and cheese, salt and pepper. Scramble until fairly dry. Fill the rolls with the hot mixture, replace 'plugs' and serve with watercress.

QUICK SCONE PIZZA   serves 2

55 g (2 oz) wholemeal self raising flour
55 g (2 oz) plain flour   **25 g (1 oz) margarine**
½ teasp salt
2 tablesp ice-cold water   **2 tablesp milk**

Blend flour and fat to breadcrumb consistency, add liquid slowly until just combined, then divide dough into two and roll or pat into thinnish circles on a greased baking tray (part-cook this before adding the topping if you prefer a crisp scone - about 10 mins in a hot oven).

Topping:: **1 tin tomatoes 1 large onion   fresh or dried herbs**
Gently fry onion in a teasp oil, add tomatoes and simmer until all the liquid is absorbed. (Make a batch of this mix every now and again and freeze in yogurt cartons). If no time for that then just spread the scone with **tinned tomato purée,** add **sliced mushrooms, green peppers, fresh tomatoes, leeks** or whatever (keep sliced **peppered salami** in the freezer). Cover all with grated **Wensleydale cheese** and return to the oven for another 15 mins.

ROAST RED PEPPERS WITH WENSLEYDALE CHEESE
(Maureen Hindes)
serves 4 as a starter, 2 as a light lunch

Pre-heat oven to 350ºF 180ºC gas 4
2 large red peppers   **4 small tomatoes**
4 oz blue Wensleydale cheese   **4 large basil leaves**
4 spring onions
1 heaped tablesp bulghur wheat

Cut peppers in half, de-seed, and trim stalk. Skin and quarter the tomatoes. Grate the cheese coarsely. Add 2-3 tablesp boiling water to the bulghur wheat. Chop the spring onions and fry in a little oil.
Sit peppers in an oiled baking dish, fill with mixture of onions, bulghur wheat and most of the cheese. Place tomato, basil, the rest of the cheese on top, add a teaspoon of oil and roast high in the oven for 50 mins.

TERRINE of TROUT AND SORREL

3 large or 4 medium fillets of trout (skinned)
a handful of large cultivated sorrel leaves
(or rather more of the wild ones)
425 g (15 oz) half-fat cream cheese
1 egg yolk   salt and pepper
Blanch half the sorrel leaves after removing any thick centre stalks and line a 1-pt mould with them. Chop the rest finely, mix with cream cheese, egg yolk and seasoning (do not use a food processor which makes too smooth a texture). Put half the trout fillets in the mould, cover with half the cream cheese mixture, repeat with second layer. Cover with foil (or clingfilm in microwave) and bake in a bain marie *(a larger dish half full of water)* for 30 mins in a moderate oven, or 10 mins in the microwave.

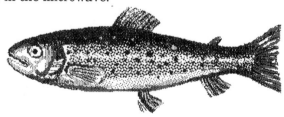

SPICED FISH IN COCONUT SAUCE
(This sauce is also delicious as part of a vegetarian dish)

550 g (1 lb) fish - steaks or fillets
1 tablesp cooking oil
1 large onion, chopped finely
1 green chilli (or 2 small dried chillies)
      deseeded and finely chopped
2 cloves garlic, crushed
1 dessertsp finely grated root ginger
1 teasp ground turmeric
100 g (4 oz) creamed coconut
3 ml (just over ½ pt) water
salt, pepper, and lemon juice

Heat oil in a frying pan and gently sweat the onion and garlic until soft. Add spices and fry a further few minutes. Add the water and the half-block of creamed coconut, stir until this dissolves into a creamy sauce. Put in the fish, gently coat with the spicy mixture and simmer 10 to 15 minutes until the fish flakes easily. Add seasoning and a squeeze of lemon juice and serve with rice.

Good *for a buffet or a picnic,*   from **Ann Gitlin**
INDIAN SALAD

6 oz long-grain rice   2 teasp curry powder
1 tablesp mango chutney   2 oz sultanas
6 oz cubed cooked chicken   1 apple
2 teasp lemon juice   1 fresh peach
5 fl oz mayonnaise

Measure the rice in a glass jug, pour out and then measure twice the volume in water and boil this in another pan. Gently fry the rice in a dessertsp oil in a casserole or pan with a tight fitting lid, add the curry powder, pour on the boiling water. Stir once as it comes up to a simmer, put on lid and reduce heat right down. Do not look at it for 15 mins, when the water should be absorbed and the rice tender. Cool, separating grains with a fork. Peel core and dice apple, mix with cubed chicken, lemon juice, sultanas and chutney. Into this mixture stir the cold rice, mayonnaise and peeled and diced peach or apricot.

PHEASANT with a Grape and Wheatgrain Stuffing

serves 6

2 pheasant
75 g (3 oz) wheatgrain
75 g (3 oz) butter
2 tablesp brandy
seasoning
225 g (8 oz) small seedless grapes
4 rashers streaky bacon
350 g (12 oz) brown rice
60 ml (1 pt) chicken stock
2 teasp cornflour
200 ml (7 fl oz) red wine
2 teasp redcurrant jelly

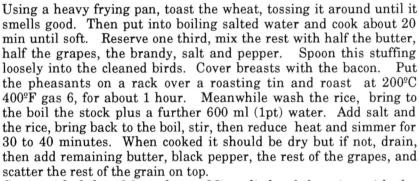

Using a heavy frying pan, toast the wheat, tossing it around until it smells good. Then put into boiling salted water and cook about 20 min until soft. Reserve one third, mix the rest with half the butter, half the grapes, the brandy, salt and pepper. Spoon this stuffing loosely into the cleaned birds. Cover breasts with the bacon. Put the pheasants on a rack over a roasting tin and roast at 200ºC 400ºF gas 6, for about 1 hour. Meanwhile wash the rice, bring to the boil the stock plus a further 600 ml (1pt) water. Add salt and the rice, bring back to the boil, stir, then reduce heat and simmer for 30 to 40 minutes. When cooked it should be dry but if not, drain, then add remaining butter, black pepper, the rest of the grapes, and scatter the rest of the grain on top.
Cover with foil and keep hot. Mix a little of the wine with the cornflour, add the rest then stir into the pan juices plus the jelly. Stir until the gravy is syrupy.

DOTTIE POTATOES (Dorothy Jarratt)

Scrub potatoes and cut in half. Make cuts across the rounded halves, about half inch deep and half inch apart, and more cuts diagonally. Put on a baking tray with a scrap of butter under and on top of each half and bake approx 1 hour. They are a delicious cross between roast and baked .

144

PORK ORIENTAL   (Marie Hartley)

675 g (1½ lbs) pork fillet
2-3 tablesp cooking oil
1 large onion, peeled and sliced
salt, pepper
1 chicken stock cube in 3 dl (½ pt) water
225 g (8 oz) can pineapple chunks
50 g (2 oz) plain flour
1 tablesp vinegar
soy sauce to taste
1 green pepper, chopped

Heat the oil in a casserole and fry the onions.   Slice the meat and
toss in a bag with the seasoned flour then add to the onion.   Pour
stock over the meat, add the chopped pepper, vinegar, juice from the
pineapple, and soy sauce.   Bring to the boil, then simmer for one and
a half hours. (This can be made the day before).   Add the pineapple
half an hour before serving.

HONEY-HERB PORK CHOPS   serves 4

4 pork chops
    Mix together --
3 tablesp runny honey
3 tablesp fresh sage, chopped
1 tablesp fresh parsley, chopped
1 tablesp ground hazelnuts
1 tablesp hazelnut oil
juice of half a lemon
salt & pepper

Grill one side of the chops under hot grill lined with a piece of foil to
catch the juices.   Turn them over and spread with the mixture.
Replace under grill until it caramelises.   Finish cooking until tender
in a moderate oven. Then transfer the chops to a heatproof dish and
pour over the juices from the foil.

WISCONSIN CHICKEN serves 8

(from cousin Jane Roeber, a descendant of the Dinsdale/Chapman families who left Askrigg in the 1850s)

8 chicken breasts
½ cup (4 fl oz) orange juice
2 tablesp orange rind
½ cup (4 oz) brown sugar
½ teasp black pepper
2 tablesp fresh ginger, grated
6 tablesp fresh marjoram
6 tablesp white wine
4 scallions (spring onions), chopped,
or ½ cup chives
2 teasp curry powder
½ teasp chilli oil
6 nectarines or peaches
yogurt or cream

Finely chop the marjoram (oregano) then combine all the ingredients, except peaches and cream, in a plastic freezer bag. Close tightly and leave the chicken in the marinade, in a bowl in case of leaks, for 1 to 2 hours at room temperature, or overnight in the fridge. Squidge it around now and again to distribute the marinade. Then put into an ovenproof dish, cover with foil and bake in a moderately hot oven 1 hour. Add the sliced peaches and return uncovered to oven for 10 minutes. Before serving, stir in cream or yogurt.

Freeze packs of the herbs in orange juice for winter, and then use a tin of unsweetened peach slices.

CRISPY CHICKEN PIE   serves 6 - 8   (Laura Hodson)

1 lb spinach (or mixture of spinach and sorrel)
1¾ lb chicken meat	1 tablesp cooking oil
1 tablesp chunky marmalade	3 cloves garlic
2 teasp ground cinnamon	2 teasp ground coriander
12 oz onions	3 oz butter
salt & pepper	1 lb filo pastry

Wash spinach, remove stalks, steam or boil for 1 minute. Drain well, and chop finely. Finely chop onion and garlic. Cut chicken into small pieces. Heat 1 oz butter and the oil, and fry chicken over high heat until sealed. Add onions, cover and simmer or cook in oven 30 mins. Check then, increase heat if too much juice, cook another 15 mins or so. Remove from heat, season, add marmalade and spinach. Leave until cold.

Melt rest of butter. Brush a loose bottomed 7" deep tin with butter, line with layers of filo pastry, buttering each sheet and allowing the spare to hang over the sides. Spoon in the chicken mixture, drawing the pastry leaves over the top one by one and brushing with the butter. Scrunch the last few leaves loosely over the top.

Cook in centre of a pre-heated oven for half an hour. Remove, and push the pie out of the tin by standing it on a smaller object such as a large tin of tomatoes. Carefully ease the base away with a fish slice and transfer to an ovenproof serving plate. Return to the oven for a further 20 to 30 mins. Serve hot.

COURGETTE AND CHIVE PATÉ

225 g (½ lb) courgettes	75 g (3 oz) cream cheese
large bunch parsley	large bunch chives
1 teasp elderflower vinegar	1 teasp sugar

Top and tail courgettes and grate coarsely. Sprinkle on the vinegar and sugar and a little salt. Toss, cover and leave at least 45 minutes. The parsley should fill up to 5 fl oz in a measuring jug when packed fairly tightly. Chop the parsley and snip an equal quantity of chives. Put the herbs in a food processor and process, stopping and starting, until they are reduced to fine green flecks.

Squeeze out the courgettes, extracting as much liquid as you can. Add to the herbs along with the cream cheese, salt and pepper, and process, but be careful not to overdo it.   Chill before serving.

MUSHROOM PATÉ

225 g (½ lb) dark field mushrooms
1 small onion
cumin & coriander seeds
50 g (2 oz) each of salted and unsalted butter
1 tablesp Marsala
1 teasp mushroom ketchup
a shake each of soy and Worcester sauce

Wipe mushrooms, slice and cube.   Finely chop onion.
Toast the spices in a thick dry frying pan, then grind until fine.
Melt unsalted butter, soften onion in this, then remove and add
mushrooms to pan. Increase heat, stir and turn for 5 or 6 min. Add
Marsala, onions, spices, sauces, and allow to become cool but not
cold. Whizz in food processor, adding the salted butter in pieces.
Pack into a lightly oiled dish and chill.   Remove from fridge 1 hour
before serving and turn out.

CREAMED CARROT AND ORANGE

225 g (½ lb) carrots
1½ tablesp olive oil
1 small orange   **sugar**
pinch curry powder   **1 small onion**
1 teasp wholegrain mustard   **2 tablesp mayonnaise**

Thinly slice carrots, chop onion.   Warm olive oil, add onion and
leave it to sweat gently a few mins.   Add carrots, juice and finely
grated zest of the orange, scant teasp sugar, and curry powder
(optional). Stir, then add just enough water to cover . Put on a tight
fitting lid and simmer very gently until tender. *(The addition of the
orange juice makes this take longer than one would expect. It doesn't
make a lot of difference if you add it when carrots are nearly done).*
When tender remove the lid and boil rapidly until all the liquid is
evaporated.   Purée in a liquidiser or food processor and allow to cool,
then add the mustard, mayonnaise and a pinch of salt, and whizz
again.   Refrigerate for several hours before serving. Garnish with
toasted sunflower seeds.

CARROT RING

Can be used on its own as a vegetable, as part of a hot buffet, or filled with chicken pieces as a main course.

450 g (1 lb) carrots   **1 dessertsp grated cheese**
1 tablesp parsley   **salt & pepper**
37 g(1½ oz) butter   **25 g (1 oz) flour**
4 tablesp milk   **2 eggs, separated**

Grate the carrots, then simmer in very little water - or steam until soft. Mash or blend to a purée. Add grated cheese and chopped parsley; season. Melt butter in a small saucepan, add flour, then milk to make a smooth sauce. Cook until thickened. Add the beaten egg yolks, stir, then mix into the carrots. Beat the egg whites until stiff, fold into carrots. Pour mixture into a well-oiled ring-mould or a souffle dish. Put the dish in a bain marie with water to come half-way up the side of the mould. Bake half an hour in a hot oven. *(Also good using half lb carrots, half lb swede.)*

149

SPROUTED LENTIL SALAD

Sprouted beans of various kinds are rich in vitamins and especially useful in winter when salad ingredients are expensive and somewhat limited. We like brown lentils best, they sprout in 3 or 4 days, chick peas are good, and adzuki and mung (which are the familiar Chinese ones).

First take a large glass jar with screw-top plastic lid and make a series of holes in the lid with a red-hot metal skewer. Put in about a cupful of **brown lentils.**
Cover lentils with warm water and leave overnight. Next day rinse them and leave the jar on its side to drain. Two or three times a day fill up the jar with fresh cold water and allow to drain through the holes. The sprouts are ready to eat when about 1" long. Transfer to a box in the fridge if you don't wish to eat them right away. Dress with **oil and vinegar dressing** to which **a spoonful of soy sauce** has been added.

Before having a food processor I think I would have avoided grating beetroot by hand for the following recipe - now it is a favourite, and keeps for 2-3 days in the 'fridge.

BEETROOT AND ORANGE SALAD

1 lb beetroot	2 oranges
4 sticks celery	oil and vinegar
1 tablesp sunflower seeds	

Peel, then finely grate, the beetroot. Finely chop the celery. Scrub the oranges and finely grate the rind of one, then remove peel and slice the fruit. Whisk up a dessertsp of olive oil with a teasp of wine vinegar and toss all together. Cover and chill for a few hours, then the orange and celery slices will be an exotic pink and the sunflower seeds will have swollen in the juice.

Why not prepare 2 lbs of beetroot while you are at it and make Borscht, beetroot soup ? It freezes well and can be served hot or cold.

BORSCHT   (Beetroot soup)

25 g (1 lb) beetroot   1 medium onion
1 medium potato
1.2 ltr (2 pts) vegetable stock (or stock cubes)

25 g (1 oz) butter	**1 teasp yeast extract**
grated nutmeg	**45 ml (3 tablesp) cider vinegar**
small carton plain yogurt	
chopped chives or parsley	

Peel and grate or chop the beetroot. Peel and chop onion and potato. Melt the butter and sweat the onion, add the other vegetables and half the stock. Bring to the boil, reduce heat and simmer 30 mins. Cool, then blend or liquidise. (If freezing, freeze at this stage). Add the yeast extract, another pint of stock, the vinegar and a grating of nutmeg. Reheat, or chill, whichever is suitable. Garnish with a swirl of yogurt and the chopped herbs.

APRICOT AND BULGHUR SALAD

225 g (8 oz) bulghur wheat	**1 bunch spring onions**
175 g (6 oz) dried apricots	**1 clove garlic, crushed**
3 heaped tablesp mint	**50 g (2 oz) parsley**
4 tablesp lemon juice	**3 tablesp salad oil**

Pour boiling water over the bulghur wheat . Leave to swell and cool for 15 mins. Wash then cut up the apricots (easiest with scissors) Trim and slice the spring onions, whisk oil and lemon juice together, add other ingredients (finely chopped) and mix.

SPRING ONION SLICE

2 bunches spring onions	1 red pepper
2 oz parsley	2 eggs, beaten
2 oz cashew nuts	2 oz butter

8 oz fresh white breadcrumbs
2 oz crystallised or stem ginger, chopped
1 tablesp tarragon, chopped
a handful of redcurrants (frozen will do)
salt, pepper and a shake of paprika

Trim and finely chop the spring onions.   Remove seeds from pepper
and dice.   Mix all but redcurrants (or cranberries), onions and pepper
in a food processor until blended, then mix in the rest (do not over
blend).   Pack into a well-greased - and if possible spring-sided -cake
tin and bake in a moderate oven for approximately 1 hour.   Turn
out when cold and decorate with a few more redcurrants and leaves.

AVOCADO SALAD DRESSING   (Jane Roeber)

1 avocado, peeled

2 tablesp lemon juice	1 tablesp vegetable oil
1 clove garlic	4 fl oz soured cream
1 tablesp chopped onion	¼ teasp salt
½ teasp chilli powder	dash of Tabasco sauce

Purée all ingredients in blender or food processor. Store in covered
container (with the avocado pit!) in 'fridge for up to 4 days. Serve
with salad, or over grapefruit and orange segments as a starter.

CARROT AND APPLE SALAD   (Eileen Suddes)

4 medium carrots
1 Cox's apple
2 slices unsweetened pineapple

1 small orange
1 tablesp lemon juice

Finely grate the carrots and apple, peel and finely chop the orange.
Chop pineapple - combine with lemon juice and chill at least 30 mins
(better still the next day).   Dress if you wish with a dressing made
from
2 oz cream cheese, 1 tablesp chopped parsley, half teasp salt,
a twist of black pepper, pinch of paprika, 1 tablesp lemon
juice.

COURGETTE AND CUCUMBER SALAD

2 courgettes
1 tablesp sunflower seeds
French dressing (optional)

quarter of a cucumber
8 radishes
French sorrel leaves

Finely grate the courgettes, then 6 of the radishes. Toss courgettes
in dressing and pile in a dish. Finely slice the cucumber and the rest
of the radishes, and make overlapping borders of these. Sprinkle the
grated radishes in the centre and scatter over a few little spade-
shaped sorrel leaves.

RED CABBAGE & APPLE SALAD

half a red cabbage
1 large or 2 small Cox's apples
2 oz walnuts
2 oz seedless grapes,
     or 2 oz raisins
2 tablesp vinaigrette dressing
2 teaspoons runny honey

Finely shred the cabbage and cut the
slices across into short pieces. Scrub
the apples then core and chop,
unpeeled. Mix the honey with the
vinaigrette and toss all ingredients
together, then cover and chill for an
hour or so.

153

VEGETARIAN DISHES *There are usually a fair number of vegetarians at our gatherings. I also find that the most conservative meat eaters make a bee-line for the following when part of a buffet table:*

CURRIED NUT ROAST

225 g (8 oz) peanuts fairly finely ground,
        or mixture of other softer nuts coarsely ground
75 g (3 oz) wholemeal breadcrumbs
225 g (8 oz) tin tomatoes (reserving some juice)
        or chopped fresh tomatoes
1 teaspoon Marmite
1 dessertsp curry powder
1 teasp dried herbs or a few chopped fresh herbs
1 green pepper chopped
1 egg
1 large or 2 medium onions, finely chopped.
1 clove garlic, crushed
1 dessertsp cooking oil   salt and pepper

Lightly fry the onion and garlic in the oil. Tip into a bowl with the nuts, breadcrumbs, pepper and tomatoes, add herbs, curry powder, lightly beaten egg, seasoning and Marmite. Mix well and put into a shallow ovenproof dish, marking the top with a lattice of furrows by pressing a spatula into the mixture.
Bake in a moderately hot oven for 30-40 mins until crusty and brown on top. Serve hot or cold. *If you don't have a pepper use a couple of sticks of celery. At Christmas put in a few whole cooked chestnuts.*

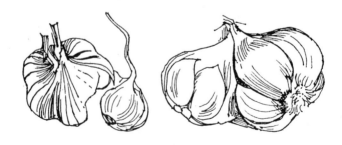

CHICK PEAS IN SPICY PEANUT BUTTER SAUCE

225 g (8 oz) dried chick peas, soaked in water overnight
2 dessertsp cooking oil
225 g (8 oz) peanut butter
1 clove garlic, crushed
1 medium onion, finely chopped
1 green pepper, chopped.
3 sticks celery, finely chopped
2 teasp turmeric
1 tablesp ground coriander
half teasp hot chilli powder
salt and pepper
570 ml (1pt) vegetable stock

Rinse the chick peas well and put in a large pan with plenty of boiling water. Bring to the boil and then simmer one to one-and-a-half hours until tender. Drain the peas - some of the juice can go into the 1pt stock.

Heat oil in a flame-proof casserole, add onion, garlic, pepper, fry gently about 10 mins. Add half the stock, the peanut butter and the spices, stir until blended then add the celery (which needs to retain a certain crispness), more stock, and the chick peas and simmer 20 mins or so. Serve hot with noodles and a salad of watercress and finely grated courgettes.

STACKED HERB PANCAKES

serves 4

300 ml (½ pt) milk
1 egg
1 tablesp melted butter
50 g (2 oz) plain wholemeal flour
50 g (2 oz) plain white flour
1 tablesp chopped herbs (tarragon, chives, oregano)
225 g (8 oz) Wensleydale cheese, grated
150 ml (¼ pt) double cream
chilli pepper   salt
1 large leek, finely chopped
25 g (1 oz) butter
175 g (6 oz) flat field mushrooms, sliced

Make batter in a liquidiser, pouring in milk, then eggs, herbs, butter, flour. Allow to stand half an hour
   Filling 1. Mix 6 oz of the cheese with the cream, salt & pepper.
   Filling 2. Fry leeks in butter, add mushrooms and fry another 3
   minutes. Season.
Make 12 thin pancakes in a medium-size pan.
Pile into a heatproof dish, alternating the fillings, sprinkle remaining cheese on top and bake in a hot oven 15 mins, or grill gently for 10 mins. Serve cut in wedges.

HOT AND SPICY FRUIT AND NUT CASSEROLE

A useful standby as all but the first few ingredients come out of the
store cupboard   **serves 4**

1 large onion, finely chopped
1 clove garlic, crushed
2 teasp finely grated fresh ginger (can grate when frozen)
1 carrot, finely chopped
2 sticks celery, finely sliced
1 red & 1 green pepper, chopped
1 225 g (8 oz) tin tomatoes + 1 dessertsp tomato purée
50 g (2 oz) each of dried apricots & pitted prunes, sliced
50 g (2 oz) raisins
50 g (2 oz) walnuts
50 g (2 oz) chopped brazil nuts
50 g (2 oz) cashew nuts
1 tablesp dark soy sauce
1 teasp each cumin & coriander, freshly ground
1 dessertsp cooking oil
Fresh or dried chillies to taste - remove all seeds and slice
(or a fairly hefty dash of Tabasco sauce)
about ½ pt water

In a fireproof casserole gently fry the onion and garlic in the oil. Add
celery, peppers, chillies and carrot and stir for a few minutes. Add
the rest, cover and slowly simmer for an hour or more (stirring
occasionally). Serve on a bed of brown rice. *(The best ones are hot
enough to make your eyes water!)*

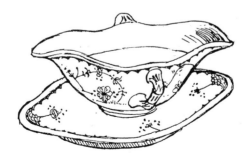

CHOCOLATE GATEAU

serves 10

Grease and line two 8" sandwich tins.
220 g (8 oz) margarine
220 g (8 oz) caster sugar
170 g (6 oz) self raising white flour
50 g (2 oz) cocoa powder
1 dessertsp instant coffee, dissolved in
2 tablesp water
2 eggs

Cream sugar and margarine, add lightly beaten eggs, sieved flour-and-cocoa, coffee and water last. Divide mixture into the two tins, bake at 375ºF 180ºC gas 4 for 30-40 minutes (or until they no longer make a prickly sound). Cool on a wire rack.

Filling / topping:
3 dl (½ pt) stiffly whipped cream
crystallised tiny pansies, roses or primroses.
chocolate rose leaves
bilberry or blackcurrant jam

For chocolate fudge icing:
75 g (3 oz) icing sugar
25 g (1 oz) cocoa powder
37 g (1½ oz) butter
2 tablesp water
50 g (2 oz) caster sugar

Split each cake in two and sandwich the layers, one with the jam, one with stiffly whipped cream and one with.....

Chocolate fudge icing
Sift icing sugar and cocoa powder into mixing basin. Heat butter, sugar and water gently in a saucepan, stirring until sugar is dissolved. Bring to boil, remove from heat and pour into sifted ingredients. Beat until smooth. (This icing sets fairly quickly so have the cake ready). Spread icing over the third cut layer and add to the pile! Swirl the remaining fudge icing on top of the cake, scattering crystallised flowers. Cover sides with the remaining whipped cream and decorate with chocolate rose leaves.

YOGURT ICECREAM

450 g (1 lb) yogurt, home made if possible
2 tablesp runny honey
50 g (2 oz) caster sugar
juice of 2 lemons and grated rind of 1
150 ml (¼ pt) double cream

Beat all the ingredients together, cover bowl with clingfilm and freeze until firm. Remove from freezer and beat again, then pour into plastic box and freeze until required.

As lemon and chocolate seem always to be the most popular puddings here is another even easier lemon icecream:

LEMON ICECREAM

large tin sweetened condensed milk
4 eggs, separated
3 dl (½ pt) double cream
juice and finely grated rind of 4 lemons
25 g (1 oz) caster sugar

Beat milk and cream with egg yolks. Add lemon and stir until thickened. Whisk egg whites until stiff, add sugar and beat until glossy. Fold into the cream and lemon mixture, pile into a plastic box and freeze until firm.

BAKED STUFFED DATES serves 6 (Dorothy Jarratt)

12 large fresh dates 3 egg yolks
3 dl (½ pt) double cream 1 tablesp rum

filling--50 g (2 oz) ground almonds
    25 g (1 oz) pistachio nuts
    25 g (1 oz) candied orange peel
    25 g (1 oz) muscatel raisins,
    25 g (1 oz) walnuts
    25 g (1 oz) stem ginger
    1 tablesp honey
    1 tablesp rum
    ¼ teasp ground ginger
    ¼ teasp ground cinnamon

Put all filling ingredients in blender and combine to a soft paste (or chop by hand and stir).   Remove date stones and pack each date with plenty of stuffing.   Put a pair of dates in each of 6 cocottes or ramekins.
Combine egg yolks, rum (or Drambuie), and cream. Pour over dates and bake in a bain-marie at 350ºF 180ºC gas 4 for 20 to 30 mins until set.   Serve warm or hot.

AMERICAN RICE PUDDING (Ann Gitlin)

1½ cups cooked rice 4 cups milk
1 teasp nutmeg 4 eggs
1 teasp cinnamon 1 cup raisins
¾ cup sugar 2 teasp vanilla

Grease a quart casserole. Scald the milk and gradually pour into the rice, stirring constantly. Add the slightly beaten eggs and the sugar, raisins and vanilla essence. Sprinkle the nutmeg and cinnamon on top.   Put the casserole in a tin of boiling water and bake uncovered at 350ºF. After 15 mins of baking stir with a fork. Bake a further 25 to 30 mins. Serve hot or cold.

GRAPE AND KIWI BRULÉE

serves 6

1 lb green grapes (small seedless if possible)
3 kiwi fruit
large carton fromage frais
6 oz demerara sugar

Wash grapes, slice and de-pip if necessary. Thinly peel and slice the kiwi fruit. Put into individual oven-proof ramekins (or a large heat-proof dish) and completely cover the fruit with a thick layer of fromage frais. Over this spoon on a thick layer of demerara sugar and put under a hot grill until it bubbles. Cool, then chill.

An alternative topping is to put a layer of soft brown sugar over the fromage frais (or mixture of yogurt and lightly whipped cream) then chill overnight, when the sugar will have melted and turned to fudge.

MINCEMEAT WITH GRAPES
(suitable for vegetarians as it contains no suet)

450 g (1 lb) raisins
450 g (1 lb) brown sugar
450 g (1 lb) sultanas
450 g (1 lb) sound green grapes
450 g (1 lb) currants
675 g (1½ lbs) apples
2 lemons
1 teasp mixed spice
half a nutmeg, grated
350 g (¾ lb) mixed peel

Prepare fruit as usual. De-pip and remove any loose skin from grapes. Add juice of 2 lemons, mix all together and either put through a mincer or lightly blend in a food processor. Put into jars. The grapes, which make the mincemeat very digestible, take the place of suet. It will keep well for two or three years.

William Mayne's CHUTNEY (uncooked) *This versatile chutney is very easy to make and keeps well. I also make a milder version (with frozen gooseberries) without the onions and spices.*

1 lb 'sharp' fruit (gooseberries, apples, or green tomatoes)
1 lb raisins or sultanas (or both)
1 lb dates   **1 large onion, chopped**
clove garlic (optional)   **a few sprigs of woodruff**
1 pt vinegar   **spices to taste**

Put all ingredients in a large bowl, cover and leave overnight. The next day mince, or mix in food processor in small quantities. Pot in jars with vinegar-proof lids. Best kept at least 2 months before eating.

A useful standby for delicious winter puddings especially if you have an apple tree are
GINGERED APPLES   *(May Clarke)*

2.7 kg (6 lbs) small apples peeled and cored
(Rome Beauty or Bramley Seedling if possible)
1.8 kg (4 lbs) demerara sugar
75 g (3 oz) root ginger

Place apples and sugar in layers *(old stoneware jars are ideal for this)* and leave for 2 days.
Place the root ginger in a screw top bottle with 6 dl (1pt) boiling water. Leave for 2 days.
Put apples and sugar in a preserving pan with the water strained from the ginger plus 2 pieces of ginger, boil until the apples look clear and the syrup is a rich golden colour.
Put back into the (washed) jars, covering with several layers of clingfilm, or into wide neck screw-top bottles, and use as required.
Serve with cream, icecream or yogurt.

SPICY PICKLED ORANGES

6 oranges
half pt malt vinegar
8 cloves
1 teasp allspice (whole)

water
1 lb granulated sugar
2 inches cinnamon stick

Scrub the oranges and slice. Remove pips and outer (peel only) slices. Lay fruit in layers in a medium saucepan and cover with cold water. Bring to the boil, put on the lid and simmer very gently - about one and half hours - until soft. Remove slices carefully, discarding liquid.
Heat the vinegar, sugar and spices slowly until sugar is dissolved. Bring to boil, then add orange slices. Simmer uncovered for half an hour. Arrange the slices in glass jars, boil the vinegar mixture until reduced by about half, and pour over to cover. Seal when cold.
Serve with cold meats. They are delicious at Christmas, and make an attractive gift, along with

SHERRIED PRUNES

Pack **pitted prunes** into small jars, cover with **sherry,** push a 2" piece of **cinnamon stick** down the side of the jar. After a few days top up with more sherry. Best after a week or two *(to serve with hot or cold savoury dishes).*

SWEET PICKLED ONIONS   (Anne Middleton)

1 pt white vinegar
3 lb pickling onions

5 oz sugar
2 level tablesp salt

1. Top and tail onions. Put in a bowl and pour boiling water over to loosen skins. Leave 20 seconds, cover with cold water, then skin.
2. Put onions, layered with salt, in a dish and leave overnight.
3. Rinse with cold water, drain and pack into jars.
4. Boil vinegar and sugar together for 1 min then pour over onions.
5. Seal, label, and store for at least a month before eating.

CRYSTALLISED FLOWERS AND LEAVES make attractive decorations for cakes and puddings. Offer a few mint leaves with after-dinner chocolates, or carry a small tin when travelling.

Suitable flowers are primroses, violets, hearts-ease pansies, borage, sage, lilac, marigold petals, rose petals, tiny whole ballerina roses, mint leaves and sweet cicely leaves. *Never use flowers from bulbs or those of the buttercup family.*

Put a walnut-size lump of **gum arabic** in a small jar and pour on a few teaspoons of **rosewater,** shake and leave to dissolve - it should be a thinnish syrupy consistency. This will keep for a long time and be ready for use whenever you find suitable flowers. *Alternatively, if you are unable to obtain lump gum arabic and rosewater (from a pharmacist) then use fresh, lightly beaten egg-white.* Thinly paint the petals or leaf all over with the gum solution or egg-white, using a small watercolour brush. (Paint a little gum on a saucer, then holding the stem, lay the flower on this and paint the back of the petals - then lift the flower carefully and paint the 'right' side, which will be partly coated by the gum on the saucer. Dip flower or leaf in another saucer of **caster sugar** and coat all over, then lay them in rows on baking parchment on a wire rack *(a lovely excuse to sit in the garden on a sunny day).* I find they dry beautifully in the greenhouse, or on a rack over the Aga. If using the tiny ballerina roses choose only the freshly opened flowers with yellow stamens. Store in an airtight tin in a dry place.

Chocolate rose leaves: Dip (one side only) in melted chocolate. Peel off the leaf when cool.

Freezing flowers: Tiny pansies or violets can be frozen for winter garnish. Scatter on ice-creams or salads just before serving .

Salads Use marigold petals, broom buds, rose petals, borage flowers, nasturtium flowers and nasturtium leaves in salads.

Marigold Pudding Mrs Hopper suggested adding marigold petals to a sponge pudding.

Damson Brandy
Make in the same way as sloe gin. (see Countryside section)

Kumquat Vodka

This recipe makes a small quantity of these miniature fruits go a long way. Wash kumquats and halve. Put in a screw top jar and fill up with vodka. Pour on sugar to about a quarter of jar. Leave in a dark place, shaking occasionally, for 10 days. Strain off vodka and bottle, then add more vodka and sugar and repeat once more, but leave a little of the liqueur in which to keep the fruit. Remove the pips and slice the tiny fruits, they make a decorative alcoholic garnish for sweet or savoury dishes.

Illustration from 'While the Bells Ring' by William Mayne.

And finally to legend. The tradition of dales hospitality does not fare very well in the first part of the legend of Semerwater. Once, so the story goes, there was a rich city beside the lake. An angel disguised as a beggar was sent away with neither food nor drink. However a poor shepherd and his wife on the hillside beyond shared their supper and gave him a bed for the night. The following morning the beggar cursed the city, saying

"Semerwater rise, Semerwater sink
And swallow all the town, save this lile house
Where they gave me meat and drink"

It is said that the bells of the lost city can still be heard beneath the the waters. One wild winter day William Mayne heard them - and later so did I. *(See 'While the Bells Ring' by William Mayne.)*

Another Semerwater legend tells of a battle between the devil and a giant from the summits of Addlebrough and Crag. The devil's stone still lies on the flank of Addlebrough, and the Carlow stone dominates Semerwater's northern shore.

Two more large limestone boulders on the shore (erratics left behind by the melting glacier) have always been known as the mermaid stones. A primitive carving of a mermaid, found some say in the river Bain (the original bain marie?) exists in the doorway of the old Yorebridge Grammar school. Surely there must at some time have been a legend about these! Some years ago my version was performed by Askrigg school; the heroine was Bain Marie's daughter, Semerlina the mermaid. The boys called her Semolina pudding.

This is her cake:

SEMERLINA'S SEMERWATER TORTE

3 eggs, separated   **110 g (4 oz) caster sugar**
the juice and grated rind of half a lemon
50 g (2 oz) fine semolina
12 g (½ oz) ground almonds

Filling
1.5 dl (¼ pt) double cream
chopped sweet cicely seedheads
(young green ones) or a few fresh
blackberries or bilberries

166

Topping
50 g (2 oz) icing sugar   **lemon juice**
crystallised wild rose petals   **sweet cicely leaves**

1. Butter the bottom of a 20 mm (8 inch) diameter sandwich tin and line with disc of baking parchment. Butter paper and sides of tin, then dust first with caster sugar, then flour.
2. Using a wooden spoon or an electric mixer work yolks and sugar together until mixture is light in colour. Add lemon juice and continue beating until thick.
3. Stir in grated lemon rind, semolina and ground almonds.
4. Whisk egg whites until stiff and fold into cake mixture with a metal spoon.
5. Turn into prepared tin and bake at 350ºF 180ºC gas 4 for 40-50 mins. Don't peep for at least 25-30 mins, (then cover with a piece of paper if it seems to be browning too much) and don't worry when it subsides somewhat - it's supposed to be flat, not puffy!
6. When cake is cold split and fill with stiffly whipped cream and the chopped seedheads, blackberries or bilberries.
7. In a small saucepan gently heat the sieved icing sugar, lemon juice and a drop of water to make a fairly thin icing. Drizzle this back and forth across the cake in wavelets. Scatter crystallised primroses and violets over the waves, and sit the cake on a plate of sweet cicely leaves.   (Alternatively add a few chopped pieces of stem ginger to the whipped cream, and scatter halved and toasted almonds on top of the icing.)

This is about the most good-natured cake I know. One day when dreaming of other things I had put two cakes into the Aga and was half way through the washing up when I found the semolina and ground almonds still waiting in their bowl. I retrieved the "fluff" from the oven, re-mixed and returned, and no harm done!

Tailpiece

TO WENSLEYDALE WITH LOVE   R.C.Scriven

Cheese goes with any kind of wine
Whatever its cost may be,
neither here nor there
vin ordinaire
or blood of the vine
from a costly line
and a noble pedigree.

> I say on my knees
> that there's only one cheese
> which goes with right good ale -
> cheers, aye, and mud in your eye! -
> and that's blue Wensleydale.

When Eve was tricked
by the serpent wise
he gave a flickering grin
as Adam was kicked from Paradise
because of her mortal sin.

> After they'd roamed the wilderness
> God forgave them, more or less,
> copied Eden with great success
> smiled and named it Wensleydale
> for the pair to wander in.

Adam invented Masham ale;
Eve repented, so runs the tale
(believe it or not, as you please)
and made the first blue Wensleydale
the only perfect cheese

(From the Yorkshire Post)

Weights and Measures

Solid Measures

Imperial	*Recommended metric conversion*
oz	grammes
½	12
¾	19
1	25
1½	37
2	50
3	75
4	100
6	175
8	225
10	275
12	350
lbs	
1	450
1½	675
1¾	800
2	900

Liquid Measures

Imperial	*Recommended metric conversion*
pints	dl
¼	1.5
⅓	2.1
½	3
¾	4.5
1	6
1¼	7
1½	9
	litres
1¾	1
2	1.2
2½	1.5
3	1.8

INDEX   Recipes

INDEX   Contributors